ANGLESEY COAST WALKS

Cemaes Bay

ANGLESEY COAST WALKS

by
Cecil Davies

CICERONE PRESS
MILNTHORPE, CUMBRIA

© Cecil Davies
ISBN 1 85284 266 0
A catalogue record for this book is available from the British Library.

Other Cicerone books by the same author:
    Mountain Walking in Austria

Front cover: South Stack & Elin's Tower

CONTENTS

INTRODUCTION

When William Wordsworth published his *Guide to the Lakes* and wanted to give a comprehensive view of "the country as formed by Nature", he asked the reader to place himself in imagination upon a cloud hanging midway between Great Gable and Scafell. Today we no longer need the poet's imaginary cloud, and to view the Isle of Anglesey, as formed by nature, we can actually hover over a point, say, halfway between Llanerch-y-medd and Llangefni and see for ourselves the shape and structure of the island; and failing a helicopter or hot-air balloon we can do this comfortably at home with the help of the Ordnance Survey map.

Anglesey is roughly square and its coast thus falls into four clearly defined sections each with its distinctive character determined by geology, pre-history and history, and though the island is twisted or tilted on the map slightly to the west, it is convenient to refer to these sections as North, South, East and West.

The East Coast is one of beaches and estuaries with the spur of the Penmon peninsula at its southern end. The West Coast offers the greatest variety of coastline including that of Holyhead Island, linked to the 'mainland' of Anglesey by the Stanley Embankment and Four Mile Bridge (Pont Rhydbont). The South Coast, bordering on the Menai Straits (Afon Menai), has least scope for the walker as much of it consists of private land or tarmac roads. The North Coast is the glory of Anglesey. Its spectacular cliffs and coves are comparable with those of West Cornwall, and no higher praise than that can be given.

This guide is therefore divided into four main sections within which the individual walks are mostly short enough to be walked 'there and back' in one day's outing. All can, of course, be walked in reverse and long-distance walkers can link them at will. This is not a 'turn-left-at the-next-stile' guidebook but aims to draw the walker's attention to interesting features of all kinds from the archaeological to the ornithological, not only on the actual coast but sometimes within easy walking distance from it.

The Welsh name for Anglesey is Ynys Môn and many places and features on the island have two names, Welsh and English. Both are given in this guide. It is courteous to use the Welsh name when speaking to local people and an even greater courtesy to pronounce the name correctly. Contrary to popular belief in England the Welsh language, though not easy to learn, is quite easy to pronounce. Once the Welsh values of certain letters are known, spelling is virtually phonetic. Many books are available with fuller pronunciation guides, but if non-Welsh-speakers observe the following basic points the resulting pronunciation will be at any rate tolerable to the Welsh ear.

Consonants

c	=	k - *always!*
ch	=	ch as in Scottish 'loch'
dd	=	th as in 'this', NOT 'thing'
f	=	v
ff	=	f
g	=	g as in 'gate', NOT 'gin'
ll		frightens the 'foreigner'. It is what phoneticians call the 'voiceless l'. Place the tip of the tongue on the ridge behind the top teeth and expel air WITHOUT USING YOUR VOCAL CHORDS. *No problem!*
s	=	s as in 'sea', NOT 'these'
		BUT
si	=	sh
th	=	th as in 'thing', NOT 'this'

Vowels

You can 'get by' with English sounds except for:

u	=	roughly French 'u' or German 'ü'. Otherwise try 'y' in 'mystery'.
w	=	oo (this is important)
y		the standard grammar books tell you:

      y = i in final syllables

      y = u as in 'gun' in all other syllables

But in North Wales the 'i' sound is used in all syllables except in common monosyllables like 'y' and 'yn', where the y as in 'gun' sound is used. Thus the Welsh for 'mountain', *mynydd*, is 'officially' pronounced 'munnith', but in North Wales, including Anglesey, it is usually 'minnith'.

The stress (accent) is usually on the penultimate syllable, eg. Llangéfni.

Note: Don't be put off by 'initial mutation', changes in the initial consonants, which often occur, eg. *moel* (hill) is often *foel*.

Hen Golwyn = Old Colwyn (the 'e' in 'hên' is long as in English 'pain', not short as in 'pen'.)

LIST OF OS MAPS

Landranger Series, Sheet 114: Anglesey (1:50,000):
Shows the whole of Anglesey in enough detail for most purposes. Does NOT show, for example, stone walls.

Pathfinder Series (1:25,000):

Sheet	733	Amlwch & Cemaes Bay
Sheet	734	Holyhead (Caer Gybi)
Sheet	735	Red Wharf Bay
Sheet	750	Rhosneigr
Sheet	751	Bangor & Llangefni
Sheet	752	Llanfairfechan
Sheet	768	Caernarfon

These are wonderfully detailed maps. Note that 752 covers only half the area of the rest and is needed only for Penmon and Beaumaris.

The North Coast

POINT LYNAS TO AMLWCH PORT

Point Lynas is the north-east corner of the island and marks the junction of the East and North Coasts. Its English name has been 'Welshed' as Pwynt Leinws, but there is also a genuinely Welsh alternative, Trwyn Eilian (Eilian Point). The Point is dominated by its magnificent lighthouse, second only on Anglesey in pictorial and dramatic grandeur to South Stack. Now automated, uninhabited and operated by Trinity House, it is the 1835 replacement (modernised in the 1960s) of an original oil-fired lighthouse placed there by the Liverpool Pilotage Service in 1779. You can park on rough ground outside the gate of its private drive and walk to the end of the Point, passing on your way the Pilot Station, founded in 1766 as a base for pilots to guide ships to Liverpool: clear evidence of the dangers of this treacherous stretch of coastline. The now empty residential accommodation grouped round a central courtyard in the manner of a baronial castle is still impressive. On the north side a wooden walkway gives access to a view of the great light with its huge compound lenses, which sends out flashes every ten seconds and is visible for twenty miles. A little below is the foghorn: remember that it is liable to emit a startling noise without warning!

Returning, walk down the road to the cove, Porth Eilian, noticing on your left the starting-points of two East Coast footpaths, one at the top and one near the bottom of the hill. There is no parking down at the sheltered, pebbly cove.

The Coastal Footpath sign is obvious at the bottom, on the right, and the path leads quickly out onto the cliffs, soon reaching a rocky inlet, Porth-yr-ychen (Port of the Oxen). Somewhere in this area, according to the map, there is a cave, Ogo'r Sant (The Saint's Cave), but I have never found it. From here also there is a right of way (but no obvious path) inland to the church, whose solid pyramidal spire surmounts its squat tower.

Worship here dates back to the 5th century, when St Eilian established

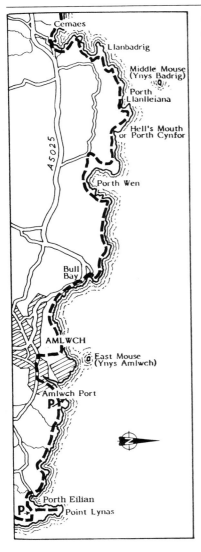

his cell, *while the church itself dates from the 12th century to the 15th, with a 17th century passage leading to St Eilian's Chapel, which is possibly 14th century. The interior is worth a visit (remarkable wood-carvings) if you can gain admission.*

Back on the coast, continue west along the cliffs. After crossing one stream, but before reaching a second, you may like to ramble a few yards inland in search of Ffynnon Eilian (Eilian's Spring). You may even find it!

This easterly section of the path is across grassy fields where cattle often graze; the westerly section crosses open moorland where you may well encounter horses. Near the headland Llam Carw (The Deer's Leap) there are some buildings. The path is on the landward side, and beyond is a hard-top road with a car park: useful if you are starting the walk at this end. This road leads down to Amlwch, a town interesting rather than picturesque. You will first reach Amlwch Port (Porth Amlwch), perhaps the most striking feature of the town, being a creek cutting deeply into the coastline.

11

The boats moored here today are chiefly fishing and pleasure boats, but two hundred years ago it was a busy and important industrial port, and in the shipbuilding yard of Captain William Thomas wooden barquentines and schooners were built, and iron boats, too, when his son succeeded to the business. Amlwch ships sailed all over the world. Letters posted from South America and the Far East, written by John Roberts (1858-1882) of Llaneilian survive. He was Second Mate of a ship out of the Amlwch yard, the Countess of Kintore, *last sighted on 15 September 1882, but never seen again.*

The boom which led to the expansion and development of Amlwch from a tiny fishing village was due to the proximity of Parys Mountain (Mynydd Parys) about a mile to the south.

PARYS MOUNTAIN (MYNYDD TRYSGLWYN)

Although not on the coast, Parys Mountain's History is closely linked with that of the port and anyone with the least interest in industrial archaeology, or even in an exotic oddity of landscape, will find it worth a visit.

From Amlwch Port follow a footpath starting at GR449930. After about a kilometre this leads to the main road. Cross this and follow a very straight track (evidently of industrial origin) to reach the Mountain. Other footpaths begin on the A5025 at Cerrig-Mân, Pen-y-lan, and on the Pensarn by-pass; at GR439906 on the B5111; and at GR439909 on an unnumbered road linking the B5111 to the A5025 at Llaneuddog. The Mountain is no longer out of bounds to walkers, but please keep to the rights of way and other well-worn tracks for safety (old shafts etc). Features of particular interest are the remains of a summit windmill, the vast crater-like hollow with its lake in the heart of the mountain, and a pumping-house built by Cornish engineers in the style of the 'scat bals' (ruined mines) of Cornwall.

The mining history of this now desolate, yet richly though darkly, colourful 'moonscape' goes back to Roman times when opencast copper mining, perhaps with the addition of horizontal 'adits', was developed on a major scale, although it virtually ceased when the Roman occupation ended in the 5th century AD. The English (and more commonly used) name Parys Mountain (with its own Welsh version, Mynydd Parys) probably comes from that of Robert Parys the Younger. As Chamberlain, he was responsible for collecting fines from the people of Anglesey after the defeat in 1406 of the revolt of Owain Glyn Dwr (Owen Glendower): the total fine was £537.7s, a huge sum in the 15th century. As a reward, Robert Parys was given this land by King Henry IV.

There is no evidence of any mining here, however, between the Romans and the 18th century, when the Industrial Revolution brought an unprecedented demand for copper (and zinc). The small companies that pioneered the mining eventually merged to form two major companies, Parys Mines and Mona Mine, and between 1768 and 1815 Parys Mountain became the greatest copper mine in the world, in some decades producing more copper than the whole of Cornwall. It was then that Amlwch Port and the town itself developed. Even St Eleth's Church (1800) owes its existence to an endowment from the mining company. Its architect James Wyatt had just finished (1799) rebuilding Plas Newydd on the Menai Strait, whose grounds, laid out soon afterwards by Humphrey Repton (1752-1818), were probably paid for out of the mine's profits, as were the landscape gardens of Llysdulas, now no longer one of the island's glories.

It is not easy today to imagine a time when some 1500 men, women and children worked in the opencast pits in what must have been appalling conditions and when the smoke of twenty smelting furnaces hung over Amlwch, preparing the metal to be shipped all over the world from Amlwch Port. The mining was in effect a kind of quarrying supplemented by precipitation. The lagoons for this purpose remain to this day.

Despite a temporary recovery in the 1830s the industry declined after 1815 and had ceased to exist by the end of the 19th century. However, a financially unsuccessful mining operation on the north-west side of the B5111 in about 1990 showed that the active history of Parys Mountain may belong to the future as well as to the past.

Indeed, that past may well belong to the future if the Amlwch Industrial Heritage Trust *has its way. The trust aims not only to preserve the industrial archaeology of Parys Mountain and other important sites, but to signpost the existing footpath network and to have illustrative boards set up 'to help visitors to interpret what they see'. It is to be hoped that the fundamentally positive aims of the Trust do not destroy the essential romance of this uniquely beautiful-ugly area. Already finds probably dating back to the Bronze Age have been unearthed, and the use of the Mountain as a dump for waste has been discouraged.*

AMLWCH TO BULL BAY (PORTH LLECHOG)

The route from the car park at the end of the path from Point Lynas leads down to the harbour road. The Liverpool Arms is facing you. Turn right, pass a level crossing and a crossroads, then take a rough lane on the right (west) inland of the chemical works. (If parked in Amlwch main car park you can reach this quickly along the road to Amlwch Port.)

Follow the rough lane, and at the second cottage go through a kissing-gate and continue to the coast, keeping straight on past a post with a yellow arrow and noticing *en route* an unusual stile with a right-angle turn in its steps. Now keep on the seaward side of a drystone wall.

A good footpath now leads along a stretch of coast intrinsically as beautiful as any of the remoter sections. (At least the industrial estate with its chemical works is behind you if you walk in this direction!) You pass a rocky headland, Graig Ddu (Black Crag), with an offshore rock. Further offshore is Ynys Amlwch (Amlwch Island), more commonly referred to as East Mouse, a name which links it with Middle Mouse and West Mouse further along the coast. A little further on there is a sort of landing-place below the path, where steps and walkways can take you close to the sea in safety.

Soon after this the 'official' coastal path goes through a kissing-gate and diagonally across pastures to another. There is a sort of rough car park here (road access from the A5025) and the path drops again to the head of a narrow inlet. (There is an equally good path keeping to the coast to the same spot.) Then up 'made' steps and across more pasture until presently the path bears inland and uphill to join the main A5025 just above a large lay-by opposite the Bull Bay Golf Club. Walk down the road and fork right to the actual cove of Porth Llechog. (There is a useful car park on the left if you follow the road round to the left for a few yards.) When weather and tide are right there may be boating activity from the sailing club. Otherwise this is a quiet spot well served with hotels (Trecastell and Bull Bay) and no longer a fishing port or pilot station with a shipyard.

Natural Arch, Porth Wen

BULL BAY (PORTH LLECHOG) TO PORTH WEN

The officially signed Coastal Path starts up a road that passes to the right of the Bull Bay Hotel, becomes rougher, and leads through a kissing-gate on to the cliff path. Opposite the hotel a tarmac drive, 'pedestrians only', joins the more interesting route from the shore, a fenced path above the rocks of Porth Llechog which leads to steps and to the western side of a remarkable house that seems to have grown out of the rocks themselves. This path leads to another kissing-gate alongside that on the official route. From here a clear cliff path, muddy at times in places, takes you dramatically to Trwynbychan, the eastern buttress of the shapely and well-rounded bay of Porth Wen. The cliffs along here exhibit spectacular slabs of richly coloured rock.

Rock pigeons may be spotted here, too, and pairs of fulmars nest on the ledges. I have seen several pairs 'staking out their claims' for spring nesting-places as early as Boxing Day. Ravens also build their large, untidy nests on large but inaccessible platforms.

At Trwynbychan the path turns south, following the coast of the bay, to Castell.

15

(If you want a 'round' walk back to Porth Llechog there is a field path parallel with the coast back to Bull Bay. It is not absolutely easy to follow in places and passes through a farm where you may encounter horses before finishing on tracks.)

To continue the coastal route, go through Castell, continue for 100yds or so on the coast side of a field and then bear left uphill. Parts of this section are often very muddy, and you may meet cattle. Don't be misled now by trying to keep near the coast! You must continue uphill to join a minor road at GR 399943. Turn right on this road and almost immediately take the rough track on the right. This soon becomes the continuation of the coastal path, dropping down to just above the Porth Wen, or Cemaes, Brickworks.

Even from across the bay you will doubtless have been intrigued by this piece of industrial archaeology, with its elegantly proportioned chimney-stacks and igloo-like kilns, fortunately now scheduled for preservation. They are worth the effort of a visit, and their pictorial merit is enhanced by a fine natural arch, while their sheltered situation frequently offers a tempting picnic spot. (But be careful, especially if you have children with you. Sites like this are full of 'Pooh traps for Heffalumps'.)

Porth Wen

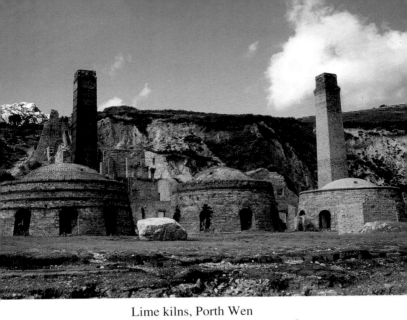

Lime kilns, Porth Wen
Porth Llanlleiana: former china-clay works

Coastal view from Penbrynyreglwys above Carmel Head (Trwyn y Gader) with Wylfa Power Station in the distance
View from Carmel Head showing West Mouse and a passing boat

PORTH WEN TO CEMAES

If you are starting your walk at Porth Wen you may well have parked at GR 399944 on the loop road and will now want to explore the brickworks already mentioned. It is worth going out on to the headland, Torllwyn, where you may see the masts that indicate a measured nautical mile. The view is good and you may think this a suitable picnic spot. (There are often horses in this area.)

Back on the main path, notice the old winding-gear - part of the old brickworks. The small cove below you is Porth Adfan. From here you are on a fine path that eventually drops down to Porth Cynfor, a narrow inlet, rockily hemmed in, but hardly impressive enough to justify its English name, Hell's Mouth. There is an awkward stile to get over here.

Although there is a public footpath traversing the southern slopes of the next headland, Llanlleiana Head, most walkers will doubtless prefer to strike steeply up to the summit where there are the remains of a Celtic hill fort, Dinas Gynfor, the most northerly fortification in Wales. A little further on, magnificently placed for the views (as you might expect), is a derelict summer-house of the Stanley family, who presumably were able to ride up the easier route which winds up the southern slopes.

There is an under-floor cavity, perhaps to keep the wine cool when the aristocrats enjoyed an al fresco meal here in this most northerly building in Wales: it is even a few yards further north than the lighthouse on the Skerries! Part of this headland is now under the care of the National Trust.

If you go down by the 'Stanleys' track, keep right at the bottom to reach the cove. (From the foot of the 'Stanleys' path a public footpath leads up to the road at a sharp bend at GR 386944. There is *very limited* parking at this point. Please keep dogs on leads across the fields.)

It is more exciting and scenically much more interesting to go straight down into Porth Llanlleiana where there are the ruins of a former china-clay works.

This ruined building has some, no doubt fortuitous, pictorial merit, enhanced by the chimney-stack on the slope above it and especially by the interlaced curves of a sea-wall both practical and beautiful. (Best viewpoint on the other side of the cove.)

In spite of the public right of way marked on the map it is quite tricky to get from the stony and cliff-flanked cove onto the cliff path again. This now traverses steep slopes above the cliffs where a slip could have what the climbing guidebooks call 'serious consequences'. Think twice before using it in stormy weather, or if you are not sure-footed. When you reach a stone wall the right of way strictly runs between this and the cliff, but many people, doubtless illegally, prefer to cut diagonally across a large field. When you reach the churchyard wall you can use a stile to go through the graveyard or continue outside the wall. Here you are all too likely to encounter untidy heaps of decaying flowers discarded by the living after honouring the dead.

The church of St Patrick (Llanbadrig) has the distinction of being not only the most northerly church in Wales, built on an ancient ecclesiastical site that may date back as far as the 5th century AD, but also of being the only church in Wales dedicated to St Patrick.

St Patrick (Welsh **Padrig**, *or with initial mutation* **Badrig**, *as in Llanbadrig) was probably born in South Wales, his father Calpurnius being a Romano-British deacon. According to legend he was captured by pirates at the age of 16 and sold into slavery in Ireland. Having escaped, perhaps more than once, he went to France, became a monk and at the age of 45 was consecrated as a bishop. It is thought that Pope Celestine I sent him as a missionary to Ireland in the year AD 432. Here he was faced with a more or less unprecedented situation: to introduce Christianity, up until then primarily an urban religion and one based on the written word in Greek and Latin, to a townless, tribal society ignorant of the classical languages. Starting with the conversion of his old master from his days of slavery, Mildu, he pursued his missionary work for twenty years, finally settling as Bishop in Armagh in AD 454.*

The tradition that connects this 5th century Welshman with Llanbadrig is that he was once saved from shipwreck here, and indeed the obviously dangerous offshore rocky islet, called in English Middle Mouse, is known in Welsh as Ynys Badrig (St Patrick's Isle).

The present church, which dates back to the 14th century, was restored in the 19th century through the generosity of one of the Stanley family, who formerly owned extensive estates in Anglesey. Lord Stanley of Alderley (Cheshire) was a Muslim and insisted that all decoration, such as stained glass, should be abstract and non-representational in conformity with the strict Islamic interpretation of the Second Commandment:

> Thou shalt not make unto thee any graven image, or any
> likeness of any thing that is in heaven above, or that is in
> the earth beneath, or that is in the water under the earth.
>
> (Exodus XX,iv)

The church is sometimes kept open in the afternoon in the holiday season by lady parishioners, and the unusual interior decoration is worth seeing.

The more recent history of this church is equally remarkable. In 1985 it was partly burned down, apparently as an act of sheer vandalism. Fortunately the 'Stanley' windows survived, and the church has since been restored. The perpetrators were never apprehended. The churchyard contains many interesting Welsh tombstones with characteristically stylised images, often of weeping-willow trees.

After looking at the church and graveyard, take a walk on the headland, Llanbadrig Point (National Trust). This is the eastern gatepost of Cemaes Bay, the western one being Wylfa Head. Unless the tide is high you can walk down from the headland into Porth Padrig, a stony cove popularly called in English White Lady Bay on account of a striking natural monolith. Beyond the White Lady leave the beach up a flight of steps. Here a fenced path comes down from the road. Use this approach when the tide is high.

Now follow an excellent clifftop path (National Trust all the way to Cemaes). This drops twice into small coves, the second being marked by a ruined kiln. Just inland from this cove is a wonderfully secluded house. Through a gate near the kiln you can follow a track to the road. Turn right on the road (which comes from Llanbadrig) and you will soon find yourself at the car park at the east end of Cemaes promenade. To reach this more interestingly, keep along the coastal path round Trwyn y Parc (Park, or Field, Point). Soon you reach a seat near the cliff edge. There is a mildly adventurous scramble from here, awkward in descent, marked 'Llwybr Periglus' (Dangerous Footpath) at the bottom. The normal route continues along the clifftop until it drops down to the car park (paying in summer). It has a National Trust sign 'Llwybr a'r Trwyn' (Headland Path). You can now walk the length of the promenade or wander on the beach. Recent somewhat draconian regulations ban dogs entirely

Llanbadrig & Wylfa Head

from much of the beach, and insist on the use of leads on the promenade. At the western end of the promenade is another car park (paying in summer) and public toilets (open in the holiday season).

CEMAES TO CEMLYN

Thanks to the National Trust there is now a continuous coastal path from Cemaes to Carmel Head (Trwyn y Gader).

Cemaes (more properly 'Cemais') has a long and interesting history. In medieval times it was one of the five principal administrative units of Anglesey (a cantref) comprising two subsidiary divisions (commotes), Talybolion and Twrcelyn, which together roughly comprised all the island north of Lligwy in the east and Llanfachraeth in the west, together with most of Holy Island (Ynys Gybi). Cemaes itself was the principal port of the north coast until the mining boom of Parys Mountain led to the development of Amlwch as a port. An interesting sidelight on health in the Middle Ages is the fact that Rhyd-y-Clafdy (GR 390942), between Cemaes and Porth Wen, was a house probably assigned to lepers in the 14th century, as none

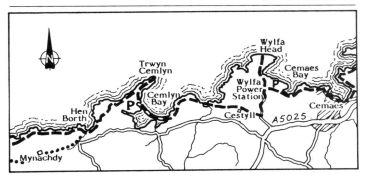

of the 200 or so leper hospitals in Britain was situated in Anglesey.

Modern Cemaes with its sandy beach, Traeth Mawr (from much of which dogs are banned) and picturesque breakwater is reminiscent of Cornish fishing villages and has become a popular resort for visitors.

From the free car park in the town centre, or from the main street, go down past the Stag Inn and follow the coast road round to Trwyn y Penrhyn where you soon pick up the path to Porth Wylfa. (There are several other rights of way leading to the coast from the A5025 between the church and the road to the nuclear power station.) It is advisable to keep your dog on a lead on land belonging to Park Lodge, a striking, castellated farmhouse.

At Porth Wylfa, an attractive cove, the official right of way goes straight across two fields to a little wood, a car park and a public convenience that will probably be closed. From here you can walk through the site of the former 'big house' (picnic tables). Alternatively from the first wall after Porth Wylfa you can keep close to the coast all the way. By either route you reach Porth-y-Ogof (Cave Bay) where a tidal island, Ynys y Wyn, has a cave through which, at low tide, you can scramble out on top of the island.

Wylfa Head (Wylfa means 'lookout') is well worth walking round. There is a good chance of seeing a seal. Sadly, the Coast Guard Lookout, from which part-time coastguards used to keep an eye on inshore sailors, fishermen and kayakers, is no longer in use. Round slate plaques inform us that the headland was opened to the public by Prince Charles when the power station was opened. The power station itself is, of course, a controversial object, particularly after the Chernobyl disaster and its dire effects on Welsh sheep-farming. Admittedly, when viewed from a distance of several miles the austerely massive bulk of the reactor-house has a certain primal simplicity not out of keeping with the cliffs of this coast, but on closer view the tangled litter of wires and pylons, not to mention the inevitable untidiness of an industrial site, destroy the illusion of grandeur. At one time it was possible to get near enough to the cliff edge to appreciate the great river of coolant flowing from vomitories into the sea at the rate of 55 million gallons per minute, but now that fences have been added to the warning notices it is not easy to find a viewpoint from which to observe this phenomenon.

The reactors have, of course, a limited life, and eventually the same problems will have to be faced as are still unsolved at Trawsfynydd. The building of a second power station, Wylfa B, as successor to the present station, would have had a devastating effect on the immediate vicinity: a new jetty at Porth-y-Ogof and a new road from that to the building-site. Fortunately the plan has been shelved indefinitely, but on economic rather than environmental grounds. A gas-fired power-station is now proposed instead.

To make itself more 'environmentally friendly' the power station provided not only access to the headland but also a Nature Trail and an Observation Tower. The former has long since disappeared - except from the OS map. From the latter it was not possible to observe anything (apart from nuclear power posters displayed inside) that could not be better observed from the top of the headland. This white elephant has been demolished and no longer has even a place on the map. More recently new paths have been opened within the grounds, though dogs are prohibited.

Looking inland from the coastal path you will have noticed some two dozen windmills. Windmills are indeed part of Anglesey's heritage. My mother (whose own mother came from Amlwch) used to say that the principal features of Anglesey were white, single-storey cottages and windmills. The traditional windmills are largely in ruins, except where they have been converted into dwellings, though one, Melin Llynnon (GR 340852) at Llanddeusant, has been beautifully restored and as a working mill is well worth a visit. The new windmills are totally unlike the old and their purpose is to provide environmentally friendly, renewable energy. They are simple and functional. Unlike nuclear reactors they could easily be demolished if they ceased to be needed. The Anglesey windmills are *three-bladed and consequently can be seen to be revolving at a steady speed from any viewpoint. Two-bladed windmills appear to be revolving irregularly when viewed from the side. The Anglesey type is better.*

After exploring the headland you must return to the car park (kissing-gate by double gates of the former 'big house'). Walk along the road to the main entrance to Wylfa Power Station; or cut through the grounds if you have no dog.

From this entrance (various notices and a bungalow with bricked-up windows) walk towards the power station. Ignore the first footpath on the left, but take the second, a track. Pass Simdda Wen (GR 531933). At a kissing-gate bear left through it and cross a field that may contain a bull, to another kissing-gate (about 75yds).

On your right now is the site of a former bungalow, Cestyll. Cross another field and go down to a single-slab stone bridge over a stream. This formerly powered the old watermill on your left (National Trust). The stream flows through Cestyll Ornamental Rock Garden. The history of Cestyll, its garden and its mill, is of great interest.

Although the present mill building and its machinery only date back to about 1840, Cafnan Mill or Melin Cafnan, has been operating on this site from the 16th century and possibly even from the 13th century. Its water comes from a man-made bifurcation in the river, the Afon Cafnan, inside Cafnan Farm, which lies on the road a bit further upstream, where a sluice controls its flow. Except for the waterwheel and its shaft, the machinery is apparently in good condition and is an example of an unusual control-system, in which the water flowed over the wheel when it was working, and underneath when it was not. References to this mill occur in the 17th and 18th centuries.

Latterly, until 1918, Cestyll House was owned by Lady Reed of Carreglwyd, Llanfaethlu (GR 308878 approx). In 1918 the Carreglwyd estate was broken up and sold. It was then that the mill ceased working, while the house was bought by the Hon. William Walter Vivian for his niece, the Hon. Violet Vivian (1879-1962), daughter of Lord Vivian of Bodmin, Cornwall (1856-1943). It was she who from 1922 onwards planned and developed the garden, which she would from time to time open to the public in aid of charity.

Through her aristocratic and royal connections Cestyll acquired a history. The Hon. Violet Vivian and her identical twin sister Dorothy were

Maids of Honour to Queen Alexandra from 1901 until Alexandra's death in 1925. Violet was also particularly friendly with Princess Victoria, daughter of King Edward VII and sister of George V. Another royal visitor to Cestyll was Xenia Alexandrovna, Grand Duchess Alexander Michaelovitch of Russia, sister of the Tsar Nicholas II (assassinated 1919).

When Violet died in 1962 the property passed through the line of her twin sister to Lady Irene Astor, Baroness Astor of Hever, but shortly afterwards the Central Electricity Generating Board began to construct Wylfa Power Station, and in 1983 she sold Cestyll to the CEGB, who have revived the Hon. Lady Violet's practice of opening the garden to the public once a year.

The cove in which you are standing is called on the map Porth-y-pistyll (Waterfall Bay), but is also known as Porth y Felin (Mill Bay). The farmhouse on your left is, like the mill, called Felin Gafnan (Cafnan Mill) and is National Trust property. This can also be reached by a track from the public road near Cafnan Farm, but there is no convenient parking. The National Trust has also acquired the coast from here to Cemlyn, one of the last links to be filled in the North Coast Path. Keep to the coast after a stone stile. The rocky peninsula on your right is Cerrig Brith (Speckled Rocks), and the promontory as a whole between Cestyll and Cemlyn is called Trwyn Pencarreg (Headland at the Head of the Rock). The farm just inland is Pen Carreg (Head of the Rock). A good ladder stile, very near the sea-end of the wall between rough ground and a field (formerly out of bounds), enables you to continue to a good wooden stile at the east end of Cemlyn. (Car park.)

CEMLYN TO HEN BORTH

Cemlyn is a Mecca for birdwatchers and is exceptionally interesting geomorphologically. Its most striking feature is its lagoon, cut off from the sea by a ridge of storm-driven shingle and pebbles, some of which were brought from the Lake District and Scotland during the Ice Age. To a degree the lagoon is artificial, its level being regulated by a weir constructed in the 1930s and reconstructed in 1978.

The fortress-like wall surrounding the buildings of Bryn Aber at the western end was in fact built as a nesting place for birds by a former inhabitant, Captain Vivian Hewitt, who managed the area as a private wildfowl refuge for more than forty years. After his death the estate was bought by the National Trust who lease part of it (since 1971) to the North Wales Wildlife Trust as a Nature Reserve. The Reserve is wardened from May to August. Before the weir was built the area of the lagoon consisted of tidal mud-flats, pools and salt-marsh.

Birdlife at Cemlyn is incredibly rich, with over a score of summer breeding birds and about a dozen wintering wildfowl; but it is the terns which are the glory of the place and in their breeding season they may be seen in their hundreds on the islands of the lagoon from the seaward side of the shingle ridge. **Please obey all notices designed to avoid your disturbing the nesting birds.** *There are also many maritime plants at Cemlyn of which perhaps the most spectacular is seakale* (Crambe maritima).

The best view of Cemlyn is seen as you approach along the coastal path from the east, as described here. The curving line of the ridge, Esgair Gemlyn, is continued to the end of Trwyn Cemlyn; the lagoon lies to the left and Cemlyn Bay to the right.

Walk along Esgair Gemlyn, keeping on the seaward side during the breeding season. If the tide is low enough you can cross the stream at the far end; if not, you must go back and walk round the lagoon by road. There is a car park at this western end also, and a walk to the end of the low-lying headland is rewarding, despite the obtrusive power station to the east.

On the headland you can see more seakale and on the east side a remarkable mortuary of limpet shells left by the seabirds. There is also a prominent memorial stone commemorating the launching of Anglesey's first lifeboat in 1828, as a result of the pioneering work of James Williams, rector of Llanfairynghornwy and his wife, Frances. You will appreciate the need for such a lifeboat if you look out to sea from the headland.

To the north-east, off Llanlleiana Head, is Ynys Badrig (St Patrick's Isle) or Middle Mouse, while almost due west, surmounted by a white marker rather like a pawn in chess, is Maen y Bugael (Shepherd's Rock) or West Mouse. From here, West Mouse is in a direct line with the Skerries (Ynysoedd y Moelrhoniaid) and may momentarily be taken as part of them. You will get nearer to the Skerries as you walk over to Carmel Head.

To continue the coastal walk: as you walk from the car park towards the headland, pass the memorial stone and turn up left by a wall to a stile. In the field, keep to the right and go over a rounded hill. This is a drumlin, of which there are several round Cemlyn. It is a deposit of boulder clay left on top of the older Cambrian rocks at the end of the last Ice Age, more than 10,000 years ago. The descent from the drumlin leads to an unnamed stony beach. At low tide you can walk below the cliffs between here and Trwyn Cemlyn. Notice a straight track directly inland, almost due south, from here, but for the real coastal walk keep on up the next drumlin. The path will bring you down to the north-east end of Hen Borth (Old Port).

There is an alternative route between here and the nameless stony beach. From Hen Borth the right of way passes north-west of the little church of Llanrhwydrus.

As far as is known this is the only church dedicated to St Rhwydrus. Very little is known of him. He is said to have been one of the wandering saints of the early Celtic church who came over from Ireland with St Rhuddlad, who founded the church of Llanrhuddlad or Llanrhyddlad about 2¹/₂ miles inland on the modern A5025. As a religious site this therefore goes back to the golden age of the Celtic Church, though the present church dates from the 12th century and only the nave survives from that early period.

The church is that of the Lewis Family of Cemlyn which goes back to the 16th century. Through marriage the family became connected with the Bulkeleys in the 17th century and later with the Hughes family of Beaumaris, through which a certain Mary Lewis inherited Llys Dulas and was living there when the copper boom began at Parys Mountain. Today the church is lovingly cared for by a few faithful families.

If returning this way from Hen Borth, continue through the farm, Tyn Llan (Church House), where the dogs may be hostile, and soon after, turn left up the straight track already mentioned, to the unnamed stony beach. If proceeding to Carmel Head, continue along the shore of Hen Borth to a stream, where a path comes down across a field to join you.

HEN BORTH TO CARMEL HEAD

If you intend to start your walk at Hen Borth, drive along the narrow road from Cemlyn past Fronddu (Black Breast) until just where the road turns sharp left towards Llanfairynghornwy, where there is a

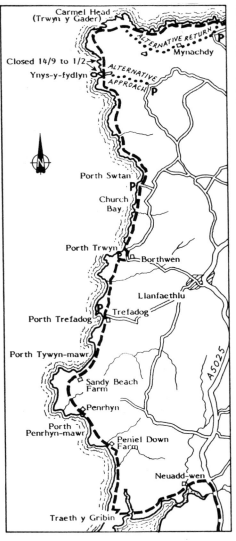

small National Trust car park on the right. Park here (GR 317927).

From this point to Carmel Head (Trwyn y Gader) there are two possible routes, so an elongated 'round' walk is available. Until the National Trust acquired the Mynachdy estate a few years ago the only way was to proceed past the cottage, Hen Felin (Old Mill), a few yards beyond the corner in the road. As this makes a good return route it will be described in reverse from Carmel Head.

For the magnificent coastal route go through the kissing-gate just beyond the car park (National Trust descriptive sign through the gate, on your right) and follow the path delightfully by the stream down to the cove, Hen Borth. Here you join the coastal route from Trwyn

27

Hen Borth

Cemlyn already described. When you reach the cove turn left and follow the coast. Observe the footpath signs which ask you to keep to the coast - and who would wish to do other, for this is one of the finest stretches on the whole island! You have to cross some half-dozen stone walls with steep stiles. Cattle are often grazed on these coastal fields. There are three named coves on this section of coast: Porth Tywodog (Sandy Port), Porth Newydd (New Port) and Porth yr Ebol (Port of the Foal). Legend has it that from a cave in one of these a secret passage once led to Mynachdy, when it was a monastery.

When you reach the more open moorland immediately south of the headland marked Carmel Head on all OS maps you will encounter two great seamarks, shaped rather like gargantuan metronomes and popularly called the White Ladies, which are directly aligned with the white chess-pawn on West Mouse - more romantically called in Welsh Maen y Bugail (Shepherd's Rock). In daylight hours these three seamarks help navigation through parallax. For the best rock scenery keep as near to the coast as the rocky inlets permit. You may well see the untidy structure of a raven's nest on an inaccessible ledge. Eventually you reach the highest promontory, the true north-west corner of Anglesey, oddly unnamed on the maps but instinctively felt by the walker to be the true Carmel Head - 'Mount Carmel of Anglesey' as Jim Perrin has called it. The sea-views down the western coast, across the sea to Holy Island and out to sea to the Skerries, are breathtaking.

The Skerries, a name of Scandinavian origin, are a group of bare, rocky islands, 42 acres of them (Welsh: Ynysoedd y Moelrhoniaid), about one kilometre long and forming the largest visible section of treacherous rocks that for centuries have made the approach to Liverpool so perilous.

One of the earliest recorded wrecks, in 1675, was that of King Charles II's Royal Yacht, Mary. It was found in 1971. Forty-one years after that wreck, in 1716, a coal-burning beacon was built on the Skerries. The motives of its enterprising builder, William Trench, were not purely disinterested but were also commercial, as he was sanguine enough to expect to collect dues from passing ships. Not surprisingly he failed, and when he died, fifteen years later, he had lost all his money.

At a later date William Morgan rebuilt the lighthouse and installed oil-lighting in 1804. More fortunate financially than his predecessor, he was paid £445,000 in compensation when Trinity House took over in 1841. The lighthouse was again modernised in 1967. In common with most other lighthouses it is now automated (since 1987) and there are no longer any resident lighthouse keepers. However, Trinity House allows the RSPB each summer to monitor and protect the birds which nest there - the arctic tern, for example, which makes a yearly 20,000 mile round trip before returning 'home' to breed there each spring. The assignment of a warden to spend four summer months on these wild, remote rocks is a thrilling challenge.

If for today this is journey's end, leave the cliffs and strike uphill inland (south-east) to the summit of Penbrynyreglwys (The Top of the Church Hill). There is no church now, but the site is marked on the OS map. The view from here of the whole island and beyond to the mainland is probably the best panorama in Anglesey. The Romans may have put up a beacon here. From the summit go down roughly north-east towards a bit of industrial archaeology, where limestone was once processed. The chimney-stack was in serious danger of falling a few years ago, but this problem seems to have been overcome, so the pair of ravens that often perch there have not lost their haunt. Then keep on towards the upper White Lady and follow a track to a small 'reservoir' and so to Mynachdy itself: the name means 'monastery' and speaks its history in its name. Go straight through the farm, across fields and down the lane past Hen Felin to the car park.

CARMEL HEAD TO PORTH SWTAN

Carmel Head lies at the north-west corner of Anglesey, the junction of the north and west coasts, but it is only possible to start the West Coast walk from here between 1 February and 14 September as the first leg is through land privately owned and used for breeding and shooting pheasants. For the rest of the year you must retreat to Mynachdy and walk by road to the National Trust car park near Hen Dŷ (GR 303914). From here it is an easy and agreeably grassy walk down to the coast. This car park is a good starting point for walking, in any case.

If the private land is open, go down from Carmel Head or Penbrynyreglwys to an obvious gate in a stone wall, through this and almost immediately down a minuscule 'ravine' and a path to a further, lower gate. Look out for fulmars on the cliffs here in the

Cave at Porth y Fydlyn

breeding season. A former path through woodland has been diverted. The new path, well signed, is dramatically exposed, with a fine view of Ynys y Fydlyn and its natural arch, but a bit scary in a high wind.

The cove into which you descend seems to be nameless, but logic suggests Porth y Fydlyn. Its principal feature is Ynys y Fydlyn. This tidal island is split in two. Either section offers a scramble when the tide permits, but is is not possible to reach the further, and higher, from the nearer. Just north of the cove there is an exceptionally exciting sea-cave with two entrances, and just inland is a small lake, Llyn y Fydlyn, which can be beautiful but frequently degenerates into a reedy marsh.

A few years ago boxes of ammunition from a wartime German transport disguised with the Red Cross were washed up in the cove and had to be disposed of by the army.

The route continues up the next headland, Trwyn y Crewyn, topped by a disused brick lookout. There is also extensive evidence of an ancient fort, but this does not appear on the OS maps. It is not as easy as it used to be to 'wander at will' on this headland, as the National Trust has put up a lot of fencing, presumably the better to

Notice between Porth Swtan & Porth y Fydlyn

South Stack, steps and bridge from the lighthouse
St Cwyfan's Chapel

Porth Swtan (Church Bay) from the north
The old bridge at Aberffraw

control the movement of grazing stock. Continue near the coast across open moorland until, just beyond a small eminence with a cairn, you go down a slight dip, cross a stream and reach a wall with a stile and a notice that the path across the next field is 'permissive' only and that dogs must be kept on leads.

After this the path continues near the cliff edge, with some stiles. Finally, after a switch-back section, it crosses fields (cattle) and ends down a short lane to a kissing-gate that brings you out near the top of a slipway down to the beach.

The cove is known as Church Bay or Porth Swtan. The English name was perhaps given by offshore sailors because the rather elegant spire of the Church of St Rhyddlad is prominent from the sea. The Welsh name, meaning in English 'Cove of the Swedes', takes us back to the 9th and 10th centuries, when Anglesey suffered many raids from the Vikings, who had established themselves in Dublin and on the Isle of Man. As late as the 1950s Porth Swtan was a lovely sandy beach, but now it consists chiefly of stones and shingle. Only when the tide is low is there a stretch of smooth sand.

The northern end of the cove is a nesting-place for fulmars, whose competition to stake out claims may be watched early in the year, even

Natural arch, Church Bay

33

Remains of wreck, Church Bay

before the breeding season properly begins. Rock pipits are also to be seen, their dark plumage showing up quite well against the ochre-coloured cliffs.

There are several eating-places. The Wavecrest and Amethyst are open only in the season. The Lobster Pot is 'gourmet' and pricey. Church Bay Hotel is about half a mile inland. The public toilets in the free car park are closed out of season.

PORTH SWTAN TO THE STANLEY EMBANKMENT

A kissing-gate on the seaward side of the cafés begins the next section of the cliff path, which crosses land recently acquired by the National Trust. This includes the first cove, Porth-y-Santes. All too soon you leave the National Trust land for a section where access to Porth Tyddyn-uchaf is barred and the path itself has been partly diverted and heavily fenced. However, you soon drop down into Porth Crugmor or Cable Bay, where a footbridge crosses a stream. After one field you are again on the cliff-edge as far as Porth Trwyn. (At low tide much of this section - Porth Swtan to Porth Trwyn - can be walked on the foreshore below the cliffs: private property does not extend below the mean high-water mark.)

At Porth Trwyn (Headland Bay) you find a good beach backed by bungalows. Unfortunately there is as yet no right of way round the next headland, Trwyn Gwter-fudr, and past two small coves, Porth Fudr and Porth y Ffynnon, so the only legal way is to follow the Llanfaethlu road to Borthwen. Do not take the sharp bend left but bear right on a narrow public road to a nameless cove at about GR 293869, and then follow the track seaward of Pen-terfyn to Porth Trefadog, a charming, almost landlocked cove which can also be reached by car from Llanfaethlu.

Leave Porth Trefadog by a lane between an ancient 'castell' (prehistoric fort) and a modern caravan park, and pass on the landward side of a prominent house before dropping down to Porth Tywyn-mawr (Big Beach), a large sandy beach, accessible by road from Llanfwrog.

From this beach the official track goes almost due south among caravan and camping sites, to Penrhyn. It is also possible, though whether strictly legal I am uncertain (there is no right of way), to bear right here and walk round the coast to Penrhyn. Here is another sandy beach, Porth Penrhyn-mawr, also accessible from Llanfwrog. Towards the southern end of this beach the path bears left (south-east) to Peniel Dowyn and from there to meet the narrow road from the Church of St Mwrog (GR 302839). You are now at the northern end of Traeth y Gribin, a vast tidal beach at whose southern end is the complex Alaw Estuary. As you walk south notice three tracks all leading east in the direction of Llanfachraeth. If you are doing a 'there and back' walk you may well use one of these on your return.

You cannot cross the estuary, but for a maximum of coast turn inland just beyond the last stone wall. The path follows the northern edge of dunes and marshes ('Rabbit Warren' on the map) and eventually reaches picturesque Neuadd-wen (White Hall). If you are returning north, follow a footpath north from here to a track on which you can choose your route back to the coast. But if you wish to continue south you must cross a bridge and walk east into Llanfachraeth. From here you have no choice but to walk on the road to Llanynghenedl. A little further on take a minor road on the right. At the main road, turn right for the Stanley Embankment. (At GR 290800 a right of way to the south-east end of the Stanley

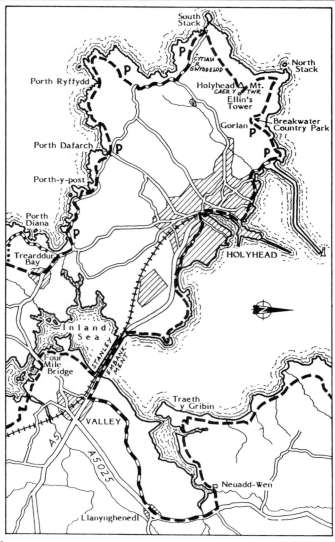

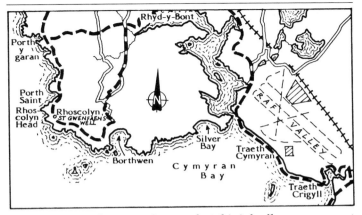

Embankment is shown on the map, but this is badly overgrown at the other end.)

STANLEY EMBANKMENT TO FOUR MILE BRIDGE

The mile or so between the Stanley Embankment and Four Mile Bridge is both interesting and picturesque. At the Valley end of the Embankment a footpath sign points you down across the railway. This is the main line to Holyhead, so treat it with respect! Immediately over the railway line you find yourself on the shore of Bae Cymyran, popularly known as The Inland Sea - for sea it really is, linking Beddmanarch Bay north of the Embankment to the open sea south of Holy Island officially known on the map as Cymyran Bay. (Neither 'Bae Cymyran' nor 'Inland Sea' appears on the OS map.)

This fine stretch of water is under threat from a scheme to build a new dual-carriageway embankment starting near the house called Glyn Dwr and cutting across to the far end of the Stanley Embankment. It is proposed that 'in mitigation' the triangle of water between the two embankments should be made into a wetland, as a habitat for birds. It appears that this scheme derives from a theory in the EU that all capital cities should be joined by dual-carriageway roads - the capital city in this instance being Dublin!

Follow the rough (private) road by the water until, just before a house, a footpath sign directs you through a small gate into a field.

Turn right and keep by the fence for a while, then cross the field to a stile. This field contains a rabbit warren. You are now passing behind The Bungalow. There is no right of way between The Bungalow and the shore. Soon you reach a damaged signpost whose function is to keep you from trespass when walking the other way. When the path close to the water is flooded follow the path on a higher level above some rocks. It is all quiet and remarkably remote in atmosphere, and may indeed remain so even when the threatened roadworks invade the Inland Sea.

On your right, before this choice of paths, a very boggy area on the right leads to a peninsula, Ynys Leurad (Leurad Island). At the southern end of this the OS map shows Cytiau'r Gwyddelod (Irishmen's Houses) - a name commonly given to Iron Age remains. (Compare the celebrated Iron Age settlement near South Stack.)

The waterside path continues boggily now until you reach the Valley end of Four Mile Bridge.

FOUR MILE BRIDGE (PONT RHYDBONT) TO RHOSNEIGR

This section of the coastal path is more interesting than the map suggests and can easily be divided into shorter 'there and back' walks if required. The low stone bridge must have replaced a ford at some time in the past (Rhydbont means Ford Bridge).

A couple of hundred yards or so on the Valley side of the bridge a lane on the south-east side is signposted as a footpath. Soon, look out for a kissing-gate on the right where the lane veers slightly left. Follow the field path straight on. It keeps quite close to the shore and aims at the right-hand end of a disused quarry. There may be cattle in this field. The path crosses a small stream, climbs a few feet to a stile at the south-west end of the quarry, and drops down to a small dam, which you walk across to another stile that leads into a very attractive gorsey area, at the far end of which is a battered ladder stile. Go straight across a field and down some 'made' steps to another damaged ladder stile. The house up on your left is Tyddyn-y-Cob (Cob House).

This can also be reached from Valley by starting down the road that branches south by the level-crossing and then taking the drive (Footpath sign) through the gate marked 'Tyddyn-y-Cob'. The river on the left has been dammed to form a lake where birds may be seen.

Do not go up to the house. The ladder stile from Four Mile Bridge is ahead, and on your left (right, if you have come over the ladder stile) is the stile on to the dam, or 'cob'.

The going here is rough until you have crossed another stile into a field. Halfway across this field is a T-junction (not visible as such) with another right of way. To the left (not obviously) this goes back on to the road from Valley. To the right it goes over a stone-slab and a very old stone stile into an area of mud and bog ('W' on the map!). Keep close to the wall/hedge and on its right until you reach a stile (sign) on to a very minor road. Go left along this as far as a T-junction; turn right here and go along down to water-level ('Ford' on the map). Do not go through the gate on your left, but follow the lefthand water's-edge track. This is a picturesque area and is the haunt of birds. Do not take either of the lanes on the left: the first goes over the railway to join the road from Valley at Cefn Llesg (literally Feeble Back!); the second is a private road to Ty'n-y-ddol (Meadow House). Go uphill and note, but do not take, the lane from Felin Wen (White Mill).

NOTE: Several variations are possible in this area, **but may not be easy to follow.**

1) Almost immediately after turning left after coming up from the area of bog and mud, take a good track on the right. This will lead you to Glan-Rhyd-Isaf (The Shore of the Lower Ford).

2) A right of way leads back from here to the road at GR 296777. Almost exactly opposite this a track leads to Ty'n-llan (Church House), turns right at the farm, passes the church and rejoins the road via a metal ladder-stile just above the ford.

3) Alternatively, at low tide, you may keep to the shore past Penrhyn-hwlad.

4) *Either* continue along the shore to 'Ford' *or*

5) Cross a breakwater (slippery stones!) to Felin-Wen and the lane back to the road.

From the lane-end from Felin-Wen continue on the road. When it bends sharply left ignore the private road to several shoreside houses of which only Ty-Gwyn (White House) is named on the map. Pass Plâs Llanfair (St Mary's Church Hall), Llanfairyneubwll on the map. At the next T-junction turn right and follow the road to

Carnau, where it becomes a rough track.

You are now walking parallel with the perimeter fence of RAF Valley and two large hangars fill the foreground. You are asked not to loiter and to beware of low-flying aircraft.

This RAF station was established during the Second World War, in 1941, and played an important rôle from 1943 to 1945 when it was the United States Air Force Transatlantic Terminal for flights to Great Britain. It is now used for training the pilots of fighter planes. The proximity of the Snowdonian mountains and valleys provides an excellent terrain for practice in mountain warfare - at the cost of destroying the peace and tranquillity sought by walkers and climbers. But the RAF repays its debt to the latter, as Valley is also the base for mountain and sea rescue, and the yellow helicopters, with their skilled crews and indomitable winch-men, have saved countless lives on both land and sea. Attempts to 'privatise' the rescue service have always been blocked, primarily because of the 'real life' practice it gives to the crews.

Keeping to the left of Cymyran (Private) you will suddenly find yourself by the water where the channel between 'mainland' Anglesey and Holy Island meets the open sea. There is a most useful recessed stone seat built into an alcove in the sea-wall. Sit here to eat your butties and contemplate the panorama of Snowdonia.

You are now about 2km from Rhosneigr. When the tide is low enough you can cut a fairly straight line across Traeth Cymyran and Traeth Crigyll, but otherwise you must go inland to the footbridge at GR 321740. In places there are also paths on the dunes - outside the RAF's perimeter fence, of course.

The footbridge is over the Afon Crigyll and to reach it you must circumvent the river's serpentine windings on the edge of Tywyn Trewan Common (Cyttir Tywyn Trewan) quite near the airfield boundary. (When the fighters are taking off the noise in this area can be quite deafening.)

Once over the bridge, if you go left you pass outside a caravan site and reach the road near a golf club. If you go left again you will soon find a footpath sign, just after the drive to Tyn Morfa. If you are not intimidated by the many frisky horses you can use this to reach the shore of Llyn Maelog. (There is a track further along, just before the railway bridge, that reaches the same point.) There is a good footpath with kissing-gates and stiles all round Llyn Maelog (except

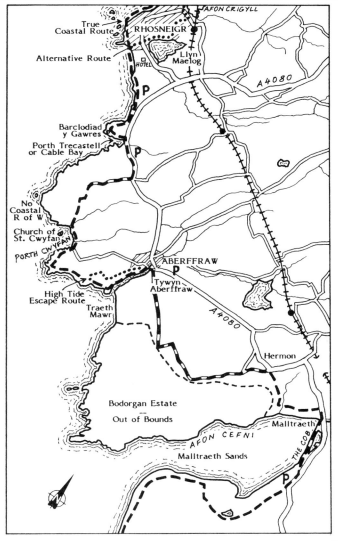

41

where the road runs between Pont Tywyn-y-llyn and Pont Rhydau-hirion). This is a pleasing walk in its own right. When you get back to the road, take the nearest path or track to the Lake Maelog Hotel and regain the coast. If you turn right by the golf club you can continue on roads or take a choice of ways back on to the sands.

For the true coastal route, however, turn right when you come over the footbridge. After crossing a marshy area you can keep between the river and the built-up town: out of season this has a deserted air. At low tide you can keep on sand and rock all the way round to the next beach, Traeth Llydan (Wide Beach). Otherwise, or if you prefer, take the last (most seaward) road to cross the built-up peninsula. Again, if the tide is low you can walk or paddle across the beach. If the tide is too high go a little way up the stream that drains Llyn Maelog, to a footbridge.

RHOSNEIGR TO PORTH TRECASTELL

Leaving Rhosneigr behind you, you can follow the coast without problems. There is a car park behind the dunes (Tywyn Fferam) which is convenient if you want to start walking at this point (for example, to walk round Llyn Maelog while avoiding Rhosneigr, and/or to visit Barclodiad y Gawres by a comparatively unfrequented route). Barclodiad y Gawres (The Apronful of the Giantess) is straight ahead of you, a shallow dome on a prominent headland.

It was taken into the guardianship of the Ministry of Works in 1958 and your reaction to what has since been done to it will depend on your temperament. It is a chambered tomb which, in the 1960s, was described as being of the Bronze Age (c1900-c150 BC) but which John Manley's Atlas of Prehistoric Britain (1989) places in the Neolithic period. It was first excavated in 1953, when it was found to have remarkable decorations incised upon five of its stones: spirals, chevrons and zigzags. Cremated bones were also found in it. It has a passage 20ft long, a central chamber, and side-passages. It was originally covered by a mound about 90ft in diameter, but the Ministry replaced this with a concrete, grass-covered dome to protect the decorated stones and to enable them to be seen by the public. You can walk into the entrance passage as far as an iron gate. (Keys to this can be obtained, against a deposit, from The Wayside Shop in

Llanfaelog. You will need a torch, too.)

Barclodiad y Gawres and Bryn-celli-ddu (The Hill of the Black Grove: GR 508702) are the only surviving burial chambers in the UK with megalithic mural art, though that of Barclodiad has more affinity with Irish megalithic art than with Bryn-celli-ddu.

The highest points of the headland are called Mynydd Bach (Little Mountain) and Mynydd Mawr (Big Mountain). The coastal right of way goes right round the headland to Porth Trecastell, or Cable Bay. (Parking.) Porth Trecastell was the eastern terminus of the undersea cable to Ireland which in turn linked with the transatlantic cable: hence its English name. The beach is very popular and you will rarely be alone here.

PORTH TRECASTELL TO PORTH CWYFAN

The only strictly legal way between these two coves is by road. Take the main Llanfaelog-Aberffraw road (A4080) as far as a crossroad. Turn right. Pass Plas Llangwyfan and then take a road forking down to the left signed 'Private Road: No parking'. This is in fact a right of way for walkers. It goes through Llangwyfan-isaf (Lower St Cwyfan) and reaches the beach between the bungalow Ty'n-twll (The House in a Hole) and the farm Ty-Cwyfan.

Much of the area you have just walked round was formerly occupied by a military camp, Ty Croes, which included a rifle range and an associated Danger Area. But there was a coastal area between the camp and the cliff. This used to be accessible, even in the days of the military camp, from the Porth Cwyfan end, without actually having to climb fences. At the Trecastell end the path round the coast had (and still has) a 'No Trespassing' notice, apparently put up by the Bodorgan Estate. In 1994 we were advised by some local people to ignore this notice "so long as the 'terriers' aren't shooting". This makes a fine little 'there-and-back' walk, because even by 1994 the Porth Cwyfan end had been fenced near Ty'n-twll. By 1996 the military camp had gone and it was possible to drive on to its now desolate site, apparently used by the RAC for rallies. Its future is at present uncertain, as plans for its development encountered local opposition. However, the fencing at the Porth Cwyfan end remains.

12th century chapel on tidal island, Porth Cwyfan

PORTH CWYFAN TO ABERFFRAW

Porth Cwyfan is another ancient Christian site and has been from about the 7th century. At low tide you can reach on foot the 12th century chapel, dedicated to St Cwyfan, built on a remarkable, circular, walled island. This is one of the most hauntingly nostalgic places on the coast.

It is usually visited from Aberffraw, keeping to the coast, but there are various inland routes also which enable round walks to be made, or high-tide problems to be overcome. From Llangwyfan-isaf a public footpath runs south-east across fields, crossing two streams on footbridges, to join a narrow road at Gate House, on a significant bend. From here it is a half-mile road walk into Aberffraw. (This is a lot shorter than the coastal route.) For the coast, walk round Porth Cwyfan on the beach. At the far (south) end the road from Aberffraw already mentioned comes down to the shore. There is very limited parking here, and, of course, a possible road walk via Gate House to Aberffraw.

Just after this you leave the beach and walk on grassy paths round the coast past tiny coves, and the appropriately named

44

Redshanks' nest between Porth Cwyfan & Aberffraw

Trwyn y Wylan (Seagull Headland) until you bear left round the main headland and find yourself on a path that now keeps at the cliff edge outside the fields. In one place, above Porth Terfyn (End Cove), you have to cross a large field that often contains cattle.

The next cove, Porth Leidiog (Muddy Cove - I think!) can be impassable at high tide. From it an inconspicuous path, oddly signposted 'Coastal Path', leads inland, turns sharp right and reaches a T-junction. If walking towards Porth Cwyfan, turn left here and follow the track to the road where you turn left again for the coast.

If walking towards Aberffraw, turn right and then take the first left. A direct footpath now leads straight to Aberffraw. You can, of course, not turn left but continue to the coast, to the mouth of the Afon Ffraw. A small headland with a stone seat offers superb views of Aberffraw Sands, the dunes and the estuary itself.

You cannot cross the water here but must walk close to it all the way up to the town.

ABERFFRAW TO MALLTRAETH

It is extremely difficult today to realise that Aberffraw was once not simply the most important place in Anglesey but in the whole of Wales. Nevertheless this is true. Even as early as the mid-6th century it was probably the seat of Maelgwn, King of Gwynedd, who has been referred to by the 6th century historian, St Gildas, as Draco Insularis (The Dragon of the Island), clearly meaning Anglesey.

In the 9th century Rhodri Mawr (the Great), a descendant, through his grandmother, of Maelgwn, ruled from Aberffraw from 844-878 AD. Rhodri was the founder not only of the royal line that included Llywelyn the Great (1173-1240), 'Prince of Aberffraw and Lord of Snowdon', but also of the House of Tudor. Llywelyn's timber-built palace, of which now no trace remains, was demolished in 1317.

At Llys Llywelyn, a Coastal Heritage Centre, you can learn a great deal, not only about Aberffraw, but about the Anglesey coast as a whole. If you are arriving on foot along the coast, as already described, you will appreciate how the tidal inlet with its access to Caernarfon Bay helps to explain the historical importance of the site.

The Afon Ffraw, from which the village takes its name (*Aber* means river-mouth), flows under two bridges, a fine 18th century humpback bridge (1731), now for pedestrians only, and a more modern, if less elegant structure able to carry modern traffic. (Car park here.)

On the left bank of the estuary you can walk down to Aberffraw Sands or Traeth Mawr, excellent for bathing and for families. The sands are backed by the dunes, Tywyn Aberffraw (Aberffraw Towans), a wonderful area to wander at will, where it is possible to feel oneself in the midst of some huge desert where a sense of scale is lost. There are in fact two actual rights of way and two roads across the dunes from the bridges.

Worth a visit, especially for birdwatchers, is Llyn Coron, a natural reservoir on the Afon Ffraw. There are footpaths to this from the main A4080 road (parking), but it does not seem easy to walk around the lake.

Although the rights of way from Aberffraw across the dunes are mapped as continuing through the fields beyond, attempts to use them can be extremely frustrating: if they are not blocked in one place they will be in another!

Nor is there any right of way around the coast to Malltraeth, though *theoretically* it might be possible to scramble around the rocky points and coves at low tide, as the land below high-water mark is the Queen's property. This is not recommended! It is better, therefore, to stick to the road: not the main A4080 but the minor, unnumbered road that crosses the estate boundary at GR 365682. After less than half a mile this bends sharply left, and then sharply right at Pen-y-lan, where there is a chapel on your left. From here the road ambles quietly through woods and fields. At Front Lodge take the righthand fork. This joins the A4080 at Bryn Merian. (The village of Hermon is on your left.) Don't follow the main road, but turn sharp right here and go downhill (extensive views) almost to the shore. (If you actually reach the shore (cul-de-sac) you will know you have come too far.) Take the last turning left. It is concrete-surfaced and actually leads to a sewage works; but you will turn right after a very few yards on to a footpath. Follow this when it turns right, and at a kissing-gate go left on a lane. You can, if you wish, follow this straight to the A4080, then turn right and walk down to the bridge over the Afon Cefni. It is more interesting to take a footpath on the right, down to the shore (second footpath on the right if you are reversing the route). This soon turns a little inland and joins the main road by the Royal Oak. Thence walk down to the bridge.

MALLTRAETH

Malltraeth (Rotting Dene) takes its name from the Cefni Salt-marshes of which a considerable area remains on the south side of Malltraeth Sands, but which were much more extensive before the Cob was built in 1815. Before that it was possible for ships, whether Viking raiders or peaceful coastal traders, to make their way through the marshes right up towards Llangefni. For centuries flooding was a serious problem. Once again, Thomas Telford (1757-1834) was concerned with its construction, which made it possible for him to run his great road, the modern A5, across the canalised Afon Cefni a mile or so south of Llangefni. Later even the railway could cross the river on a viaduct only a few hundred yards inland from

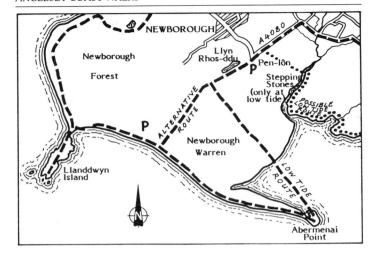

Malltraeth.

The remaining marshes and dunes, and Malltraeth Pool between the Cob and the coastal road, provide habitats for many birds and constitute part of the National Nature Reserve. Small wonder that Charles Tunnicliffe, the famous Macclesfield wildlife artist, chose Malltraeth as his home from 1947 until his death in 1979. Many of his works may now be seen in the Oriel, or Art Gallery, outside Llangefni.

MALLTRAETH TO ABERMENAI POINT

Walk south along the Cob between the sands and Malltraeth Pool. This is particularly rewarding by low tide and afternoon sun. You will need your binoculars to appreciate fully the variety and density of the bird population. At the southern end of the Cob there is a car park on the edge of the forest.

Within the forest there are several rights of way and a maze of footpaths and forestry tracks where in fact you can wander at will, pleasantly but confusingly. For the 'true' coastal route keep as far to the right as possible, south, close to the fence dividing the forest

Ynys Llanddwyn with cross and old lighthouse

from the salt-marsh. When the forest edge turns right (west) follow this. Eventually you can walk along the sands above high-water mark or just inside the forest. If you do the latter, be sure to take a path right at GR 392637 on to the sands.

Llanddwyn Island is not strictly an island, as it is cut off from the mainland only by an exceptionally high tide. You will find a main track down the centre, and more interesting and picturesque paths on both coasts. Notices relating to dogs are not entirely consistent with each other, but if you have a dog, do try to obey them, especially when birds are nesting on the ground. You will find sandy beaches and an enclosure where Soay sheep graze (see Newborough below). The largest offshore rock betrays by its name, Ynys yr Adar (Rock of Birds), that there are plenty of birds to be seen. And do pause to enjoy the views of Snowdonia and the Lleyn Peninsula.

After visiting the island continue along the beach, here called Ro Bach. After about 1^1/$_2$ miles, at GR 405633 you reach the path from the principal car park (paying). There are public conveniences here. To reach this by road, which is what the vast majority of visitors in cars do, turn south-west at a crossroad in the middle of Newborough village.

From here it is a good 4km to Abermenai along the beach: a walk not to be underestimated! From Abermenai Point you are looking across the Menai Strait at its narrowest. Opposite you to the south is Fort Belan, and looking west-north-west you can see Caernarfon Castle, the grim fortress from which Edward I sought to control Anglesey as well as the mainland of Gwynedd. It is worth timing this walk by your tide tables, for the rights of way from here are straight lines across tidal sands, Traeth Abermenai. Of the two marked on the map the easier to follow, and the more likely not to be flooded, is that which is a few degrees left (west) of the other. There is an occasional post as waymark but generally you must aim at some fire-fighting 'spades' above the beach (binoculars useful). This Traeth Abermenai experience is noteworthy, comparable with walking Morecambe Bay, but less dangerous. However, if the tide is too high, you can walk very agreeably and with a similar sense of remoteness, along the north-east side of Braich Abermenai and then turn north-east along the shore. It is also possible to pick your way through the area marked Penllyn Pysgod on the map - but this is not strictly within the conservancy's rules!

Having crossed the sands you must now carefully follow a line of poles that keeps you on a right of way across the dunes. You will feel here a wonderful sense of wilderness even though you are less than a kilometre from 'civilisation'. After about 1^1/$_2$km you reach a gate and a T-junction. If you go left you have a path, much of it along the forest edge, back to the coast. If you go right you will soon reach the car park near Llyn Rhos-ddu (Black Heath Lake) where there is a bird-hide. A short road leads to a sharp bend on the A4080 at GR 429650.

NEWBOROUGH

The whole area from Malltraeth to Abermenai Point is historically one of the most interesting on the island. Newborough Forest is the most extensive forested area, Newborough Warren the wildest area of unspoilt nature and one of the six most important dune areas in Britain; Llanddwyn Island is a unique feature.

It is possible that it was at Abermenai, the most southerly tip of Anglesey, that the Romans invaded Anglesey, first under C.

Suetonius Paulinus in AD 60 and later under Agricola in AD 78. Suetonius is said to have had a huge army of perhaps 10,000 soldiers and mercenaries, as well as cavalry. The foot-soldiers are said to have been taken across in flat-bottomed boats brought from Chester, while the horses swam.

Tacitus (cAD 55-120), the distinguished Roman historian, wrote a vivid and much quoted description of the landing which has been used as evidence that the main objective of the invasion of Anglesey was the destruction of Druidism, but Peter Salway in his authoritative *Roman Britain (Oxford History of England Vol.1A)* effectively argues against this view. Suetonius was unable to consolidate the occupation of Anglesey because of the uprising led by Boudicca (commonly and incorrectly known as Boadicea), warrior-queen of the Iceni, which he suppressed with great slaughter. Eighteen years later Agricola, Tacitus' father-in-law, completed the subjugation of Anglesey.

Newborough itself was originally called Rhosyr, a name preserved in that of the Civil Parish. 'Newborough' is a purely English name, the Welsh version 'Niwbwrch' being a mere transliteration.

In the 13th century, Llanfaes, just north of the modern Beaumaris, was a place of some importance, but after its inhabitants had supported the rebellion of Madog in 1294, Edward I destroyed the manor and the town, set about building a new castle at Beaumaris, and in 1303 forcibly transferred the inhabitants to Rhosyr, changing its name to Newborough.

After an all too brief period of initial prosperity Newborough suffered a series of terrible storms which buried much of it under the sands. Only the tough marram grass checked their movement, and Elizabeth I actually brought in a law protecting the plant. But the marram grass was also the basis of a local cottage industry: weaving mats and making brushes. As late as 1913 a matmakers' co-operative was founded, but the industry was on the way out by the 1930s.

Cattle and sheep are grazed on the dunes, now known as Newborough Warren or Tywyn Niwbwrch, and despite the great myxomatosis epidemic of 1954 many rabbits survive in this favourable habitat, which, together with Llanddwyn Beach and Island, form a National Nature Reserve.

About 2,000 acres of the dunes was planted as forest in 1948, after the Second World War. Though initially a commercial venture Newborough Forest has resulted in some ecological gains, preventing the spread of the dunes and coastal erosion, and it is a Site of Special Scientific Interest. In the part of the forest inland from the A4080 there is a 10-acre lake, Llyn Parc Mawr (Big Park Lake), with hides, deliberately created in 1987 as a habitat for birds.

Finally, in this richly varied area, there is Llanddwyn Island, Ynys Llanddwyn. Llan Ddwyn, from Llan Dwynwen, the Church of St Dwynwen, celebrates a female saint who is supposed to have built an oratory here in the 5th century, after an unhappy love affair.

THE LEGEND OF DWYNWEN

'Dwyn the Pure' was one of 24 daughters of Brychan, saint and prince, who had promised her hand in marriage to a suitor. She therefore rejected her lover Maelon and prayed that her love for him should cease. This was achieved, but only through a potion that turned the unfortunate Maelon into a block of ice. Dwynwen was then granted three wishes: that Maelon should be thawed out, that she should not marry anyone else, and that she should become the patron saint of lovers. Her well on Llanddwyn Island became a place of pilgrimage for lovers who wanted to know whether their partners were faithful. Apparently the method of divination was to study the movement of small fish in the well. The cult became very popular and so much money was left at the shrine that the monastery responsible for it became the richest in the Bangor Diocese, and in the 16th century a church, now a picturesque ruin, was built on the site. Two later crosses also celebrate St Dwynwen, one Latin and one Celtic (1903). The Latin cross gives the date of her death as AD 415. St Dwynwen's Day, treated by some Welsh lovers as an alternative to St Valentine's Day, is 25 January.

In 1800 a Beacon was built (Twr Bach: Little Tower), but this was superceded in 1845 by a lighthouse (Twr Mawr: Big Tower) reminiscent of an Anglesey windmill. Here also from 1826 was the base of the trustees of Caernarfon Harbour for pilots who guided ships over the bar, and also ran a lifeboat service (later taken over by the RNLI). In the 50 years from 1853 to 1903, 101 lives were saved. You can see the cottages, now museumised, where the pilots and their families lived.

Holy Island: Ynys Gybi

STANLEY EMBANKMENT TO HOLYHEAD (CAER GYBI)

From the south-east end of the Stanley Embankment you can continue south on the 'mainland' of Anglesey, but this is where you can cross the Embankment to explore Holy Island (Ynys Gybi), and especially its northern and, on the whole more rewarding, half. The Embankment was the work of Thomas Telford, who at the same time (about 1812) built the modern A5 as a toll road from Menai Bridge to Holyhead. At the north-west end of the Embankment one of Telford's Toll Houses, now a café, marks the entrance to a large car park at Penrhos, formerly a seat of the Stanleys. From the car park the coastal path goes due north, and it is worth going right out to the end of the headland, Gorsedd-y-penrhyn (Throne Cape). It is only 18m above sea level, but stone seats (Thrones?) enhance it as a viewpoint. The offshore rocks have picturesque names like 'Bird Rock' and 'Half-tide Rock'.

Further along the coast you will see a ruined boathouse and, more interestingly, a battery, dating from the Napoleonic Wars. The whole area is now a bird reserve, with birds of many kinds both in summer and in winter. For a round walk you can return to the car park by a track parallel with and close to the A5, or by one of several wooded inland paths.

To continue the coastal walk, avoid the busy A5 by keeping to the minor road between it and the shore, Penrhos Beach (Traeth Penrhos), and you will soon find yourself in Holyhead (Caer Gybi: Cybi's Castle), the largest town in Anglesey.

The Romans built a fort here in about the 3rd century AD. It surrounds the 15-16th century church, which itself is on the site of the monastery founded in AD 54 for St Cybi by the Christian King Maelgwyn Gwynedd. The entrance through the Roman Wall is medieval. As early as the 17th century Holyhead had become a principal port for the passage to Dublin. The old harbour, sheltered by Salt Island (Ynys Halen), was redesigned when Thomas Telford was building the modern A5.

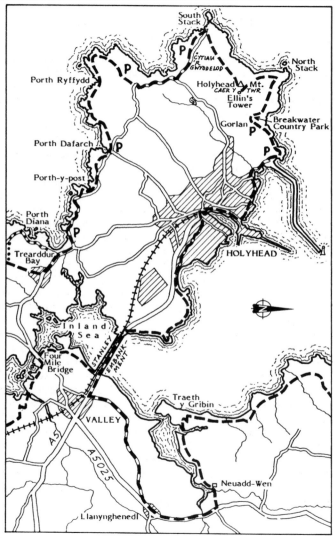

HOLYHEAD TO HOLYHEAD MOUNTAIN &
SOUTH STACK

Leave Holyhead by the Promenade, whether by car or on foot, pass the Marina - formerly a Trinity House depôt where all the types of buoy used around the coast were stored - and take the road forking left, the upper road. There are sleeping policemen along here, so beware, if driving. Where the road turns sharp left there is a small car park on the right, and a 'Coastal Footpath' sign. The path so indicated takes you round a low headland, with a small island, Ynys Wellt, and leads you to the Breakwater Country Park. But first you may want to investigate the $1^{1}/_{2}$-mile long breakwater itself, that stretches like a pulled-out letter Z from Soldiers' Point and protects the New Harbour from westerly and northerly gales. It was built between 1845 and 1873 from the quarry which has now been developed as a Country Park, the tramway down which the stone was brought being the line of the road you are now using, after the sharp left turn. If you decide to walk along the promenade that tops the breakwater, remember that it really *is* $1^{1}/_{2}$ miles (2.4km) long and without special points of interest - save when in storms the waves break over it spectacularly and dangerously - and that if you reach the lighthouse at its tip you have no choice but to retrace *all* your steps.

You can drive to the Country Park in the old quarry (ample parking), but if you are walking, and don't want to go round the headland, take the footpath on the left of the tramway road. This soon crosses the road on a bridge and passes two interesting old magazines for explosives for the quarry. The older and larger is open and double-vaulted. The green lane you are now on continues to a gate (left) or stile (right) at the Country Park. The path round the headland is almost level and also leads to the stile, or by forking left, to the gate. The Country Park has toilets, a pond or small lake, seats and illustrations of the old quarrying industry.

Holyhead Mountain is criss-crossed with paths and there are many points of access, several being from the Breakwater Country Park. It may be helpful to list these:

A. To the North

1. The most obvious route goes through a kissing-gate and up a rough track (passable by suitable vehicles). This goes to North Stack.

2. Through the field to the right of the start of (1). This leads to a clifftop 'nest', whence you can continue on vague trods to a disused magazine. From this you can go up, away from the sea, to join -

3. Fork right off (1) when it has ceased to climb steeply. No vehicles are possible on this and it also goes to North Stack.

4. Start on (1) and at the quarry edge go sharp left on a footpath (not very obvious) that bears left above the quarry and goes uphill quite steeply. At the first major 'crossroads' the righthand path leads to the north-east entrance of the ancient fort, Caer-y-Twr (Tower Castle), that crowns the summit. 17 acres are defended by a drystone wall which supplements the steep slopes. The wall is seen at its best on the north side, where it is 13ft wide at its base and 10ft high at its maximum. The fort is regarded as of the Iron Age, c150 BC - AD c385, and thus also of the time of the Roman occupation. It was probably used for defence *against* the

Iron Age village near South Stack

Romans, though there are said to be the ruins of a Roman beacon or watch-tower within it.

5. On the level section of (1), much further on, a path, not easy to spot, goes sharply back to the left. It is a picturesque route and leads by various ways to the summit.

B. To the South

1. A path to the left of all parts of the park leads to roads south of the mountain. To be avoided.
2. Signposted, up a spur between two quarry areas. This leads to the top of the village of Gorlan. Don't be tempted to turn sharp right (that path peters out) but walk down the village.

    a) Just at a very sharp bend left in the road, take a path uphill to the right. This leads to a path which contours the southern face of the mountain.

    b) Keep on the road to just below the sharp bend, then take a footpath on the right down to a road. Follow this south-west in the direction of Henborth until you find on the right a gated track that says it goes only to Castell. You may walk up here to a hairpin bend right when signs direct you straight up the heather on a path of varying quality until you meet, unmistakably, path (a).

Let us return to North Stack by one of the paths already mentioned. The fog-horn formerly here has been transferred to South Stack and is now automated and controlled from Holyhead, but the fog-horn keeper's house, now privately owned, is still there.

Before automation the keeper was glad to serve you a cup of tea as you sat in his cosy, old-fashioned sitting-room by an open fire with the kettle singing on the hob. He would also open up the explosives magazine of 1861 and show you the copper tools used for opening the boxes and the felt overshoes that had to be worn. He might even sound a deep 'pip' on the fog-horn. Before the fog-horn was constructed a gun was fired in fog to warn shipping. There were strict limits on the amount of explosive that might be taken from the magazine at any one time.

While you are down by the fog-horn building take a look at the vast sea-cave whose enormous roof is one of the big challenges to extreme rock-climbers: the whole seacliff area of Gogarth Bay is a mecca for rock-climbers, who must normally abseil down to sea-level before even starting to climb. One of the most famous is the romantically named Dream of White Horses. Just above the old keeper's house a throne-like rock has been painted with a back and legs and the initials G.R.P.

From North Stack you can go straight up to the summit of the mountain. Be careful to avoid minor paths to the right: these lead simply to the tops of rock-climbs.

(NOTE: The name North Stack strictly applies to the small island, Ynys Arw, just west of the headland.)

After the initial steep section of path you encounter the ruins of a small building and enclosure, a good picnic spot. Then, after dropping to a broad saddle you climb very steeply up to the summit (trig point). Notice the information signs just below the wall of the fort. (No real entrance here, just a scramble.)

The views in all directions are magnificent - not only virtually the whole of Anglesey, the Mountains of Snowdonia and the Lleyn (Welsh: Llyn) Peninsula can be seen but even, it is alleged, Ireland and the Isle of Man if the weather is clear enough - and all this from a mountain a mere 715ft high!

You can also reach the summit from the traversing track from Gorlan on the south side. This goes towards an active quarry, but keeps to the right of this, rises and then drops. This side of the mountain is craggy and attracts rock-climbers; but if you take a minor track on the right just before the crags become impassable for walkers (an obvious 'abseiling' slab is a noticeable feature) this track develops into a slightly scrambly way to the summit.

From the summit you cannot miss the wide paths and vehicular tracks which lead past the rather obtrusive telecommunications establishment towards South Stack. Alternatively, take a path just opposite the scrambly path by the abseiling slab. This leads past some cottages and past the finely excavated and preserved Iron Age village called Cytiau'r Gwyddelod (Huts of the Irish), for no clear historical reason. The entrance to this from the road is just opposite the RSPB car park.

To avoid road-walking there are two good paths, one wide, from the RSPB car park to Elin's Tower (Twr Elin), a white and obvious landmark. This, on its perfectly selected site, was one of the many 'summer-houses' of the Stanleys of Alderley Edge, one of the greatest Anglesey landowning families, and now an RSPB Centre, with displays, telescopes and ideal views of the cliffs where thousands of guillemots and razorbills breed every year.

Here too is the splendid South Stack lighthouse on its island, Ynys Lawd, connected with the mainland by its slender suspension bridge (built 1827, replaced 1964) at the foot of the steep steps.

In 1984 the lighthouse was automated and access across the bridge was closed to the public. However, in 1997, through the co-operation of the RSPB, Trinity House and the Countryside Council for Wales, Ynys Lawn was reopened for long summer seasons; exhibitions are mounted in the lighthouse building by the three co-operating bodies and tours of the lighthouse tower established. The suspension bridge had become too weak for public use and had to be replaced. This delayed the opening until June 1997.

A charge is, of course, made, but visits to Elin's Tower continue as usual.

Of course, Holyhead Mountain can be, and more usually is approached from this side, and both North Stack and the Breakwater Country Park can be reached without actually ascending the mountain.

SOUTH STACK TO TREARDDUR BAY

No doubt the easiest way to visit South Stack, Elin's Tower, Cytiau Gwyddelod and Holyhead Mountain is from the RSPB car park (GR 211818) or one of those nearer the end of the road, including one by the café. There are toilets by this road also. Sadly for the walker there is so far no path from Pen-las (Blue Head) Rock (GR 207816) at the south edge of the RSPB Reserve, to the boundary of Penrhosfeilw RSPB Reserve just beyond Porth-y-Gwyddel (Irishman's Port), in other words, for the whole coastline of the large bay called Abraham's Bosom. So you must use the road. At the T-road junction just below Henborth a permissive path leads to a tiny cove reached down steep steps, and to a 'viewpoint' above another. The only possible parking place has been blocked off with boulders.

Turn right at the T-junction, and to get back to the coast, take a narrow road on the right just past a right-angle bend left. There is a cul-de-sac sign but no other. The road passes Gors Goch (Red Bog)

Climbers learning rope techniques, Penrhosfeilw

and leads to a rough car park (GR 216804) and the RSPB Penrhosfeilw Bird Reserve. There are many ways from here to the coast, all of them delightful. Indeed, this is probably the most exhilarating area on Holy Island, and a blaze of colour when gorse and heather are in flower. To include a maximum of coast take a path sharp right at the end of the road, just where the car park begins. It can be overgrown sometimes. This takes you to a coastal path, with a view all the way of South Stack and Holyhead Mountain. Follow the coast past Porth-y-Gwin (perhaps 'Wine Port': does this refer to smuggling in the past?) and round Penrhyn Mawr (Big Cape). Several tracks from the car park join the coast in places. The offshore rocks to the south are Ynysoedd y Ffryddiau.

This superbly rocky coast is popular with fishermen and is also much used by the helicopter teams from RAF Valley for practising air-sea rescue. If you see a 'casualty' inaccessibly awaiting rescue from the rocks, make sure, before rushing to raise an alarm, that he hasn't been 'planted' there. If you are fortunate you may see an intrepid winchman at work - and be thankful that attempts to privatise this wonderful service a few years ago, failed. There are plenty of birds, too, and here you may still be thrilled by the song of the lark ascending.

The next major feature is Porth Ruffyd (thus on OS map) a deep inlet reached down a long and well-constructed flight of steps. Near the bottom, on the rough slope to the left of the steps, is a small plinth with the following sign (in Welsh and English, of course):

Porth Rhuffydd

The Porth Rhuffydd Lifeboat Station saw service between 1891-1904. The RNLI lifeboat was the NORBURY. A 34ft long 3½ ton pulling and sailing lifeboat. She had 10 oars and a crew of 13.
The cost of constructing the station was £1,320 and the lifeboat construction cost £436.
Service 1891-1904
Launches 14. Saved 1 vessel. Saved 0 lives
In 1904 the station closed and cover provided for this part of the coast by the new steam lifeboat at Holyhead.
In 1997 the lifeboat station winch was transferred to Breakwater Country Park.

Until the lifeboat station was demolished early in 1997 it constituted an ugly and slowly disintegrating ruin, whose chimney-stack, however, suggested that it had seen better days. From here is the shortest route back to the car park.

The next section of cliffs has several deep inlets where educational groups practise rock-climbing. Here also, a pair of peregrines sometimes nest. After a few hundred yards the most southerly point of the reserve is a tidal island separated from the shore by a deep cleft. As one might expect, it is the site of an ancient fort. At low tide it should be possible for a fit and active person to scramble across, but the rock is friable and I am *not* recommending the reader to try.

The view from all this coast is magnificent. The whole coast past Trearddur Bay as far as Rhoscolyn Beacon and the Lookout on the headland is clearly seen. Surprisingly that headland cuts off the view of the main Anglesey coast right down to Abermenai, but in compensation the whole of the Lleyn Peninsula is visible, even as far as Bardsey Island if the weather is clear enough.

A few hundred yards beyond the island fort you reach a stone wall with a stile. This marks the end of the RSPB Reserve, and the road that comes down by the wall gives the last opportunity for a round walk. Turn left at the first house. There is a choice of two paths on the left: the first (often boggy) leads back to the boathouse;

the second to the car park.

Continuing along the coast it is worth while visiting the top of Graig Lwyd (Grey Rock). Beyond it several little paths lead down to a small terrace above a little beach which can be reached by a scramble at low tide. Beyond the next stile, go down to a nameless inlet with a small beach and a miniature waterfall.

The next leg takes you to Porth Dafarch. First comes a caravan park ingeniously laid out on sloping ground. A footpath on the seaward side leads to the beach. Notice a curious building below you on the right and the remains of steps cut out of the rock - probably all that is left of the attempt to develop Porth Dafarch as a port for Irish packets, before Holyhead harbour was built. There is parking (charged in season) and public toilets (also seasonal!). The sands are popular with children and riders, and the narrow bay popular for kayaks and small inflatables.

A plaque by the path commemorates the author of the hymn *Rock of Ages*.

After Porth Dafarch the coastal route becomes scrappy. Walk round the first headland, then inland towards the road: either straight up to the road, then past a house with a notice 'Alsation' (*sic*) Loose', then through a gap in the wall to a little cove below a house, and roughly over to Porth-y-Post. Alternatively, when leaving the headland, go right at the last wall before the road; after 50yds go over a stile into a field, then 100yds to a stile on to the cliff path again. (If in difficulty, stick to the road.) After Porth-y-Post there is one more headland with a path outside a fence. After this there is no choice but road-walking into Trearddur Bay. Naturally beautiful, this bit of coast is disfigured by a hodge-podge of hotels and holiday houses, many evidently built in days when planning regulations were less restrictive.

This is the narrowest point of the island, only half a kilometre across from sea to sea, effectively dividing it into two distinct sections. We therefore begin our exploration of the southern half here, at Trearddur Bay.

TREARDDUR BAY TO RHOSCOLYN
(See map p37 for the beginning of route)

At the southern end of the main beach, opposite the police station, a road goes to the right past Porth Diana and Porth Castell. These are privately owned, with various restrictions on use. The road leads you among trim houses and bungalows, ending abruptly at the edge of a caravan park. Although the land between here and Ravens Point is private, there are some concessions to walkers' access, but these are barely worth finding.

Although this road is actually the nearest to the coast it is so built up that you may well prefer to walk about a quarter of a mile along the main road to Valley, past a track leading only to a caravan park, to a no-through road that begins unpromisingly in another built-up area, but continues into more open country. Where this road reaches the boundary of the caravan park mentioned in the previous paragraph there is some parking space, useful if you are using a car to start a walk here, avoiding as much road-walking as possible. The caravan park is unpleasant from a walker's point of view, and you will want to get through it quickly, keeping to the rules laid down on its notices.

After the caravan park, at Porth-y-garan (Heron Cove) you enter upon as fine a stretch of coast as any in Anglesey. A landmark is a small tarn. Notice that a path from the east joins the coastal path about here. We shall refer to it again. The coastal path continues,

Natural arch, near Rhoscolyn

well trodden, past the fine natural arches Bwa Du and Bwa Gwyn (Black Arch and White Arch). At Porth Saint, don't be tempted inland but keep round Rhoscolyn Head to Porth Gwalch (Hawk Cove) where you turn a few yards inland by St Gwenfaen's Well (Ffynnon Gwenfaen) which was once believed to relieve mental disorders. The path now runs straight, parallel with the general line of the coast. The Coastguard Lookout (no longer in use) is a good viewpoint. Notice the dangerous offshore rocks, Maen yr Esgyll, Maen-y-frân and Maen y Sais, and especially the group of rocks, Ynysoedd Gwylanod (Seagull Islands), crowned with Rhoscolyn Beacon.

These rocks, as the beacon suggests, have constituted a danger to shipping, and there is a grave marked 'TYGER Sept 17th 1819', commemorating a heroic dog of that name who died in rescuing the crew of a ketch bound for Liverpool.

The final stages of this path to the almost land-locked cove of Borthwen (popularly referred to as Rhoscolyn) twists its way among holiday houses, and even through someone's garden. There is very limited parking at Borthwen, which is beloved of the boating community.

This is in some sense journey's end for coastal walkers, and what follows is a brief account of what we might call 'local walks'.

WALKS NEAR RHOSCOLYN

On the south coast of Holy Island from Borthwen to Silver Bay there is no right of way but the owners of Silver Bay Caravan Park permit you to walk. You are not permitted to walk inland through the caravan park but there is a right of way through a little wood. This leads on tracks to a narrow lane. Keep left of a wood, Coed Tan-y-bryn (The Wood under the Hill). Having passed this you may fork left to Ty-du (Black House), pass this, and join a right of way back to Borthwen. Further on another right of way leads to Ty-woods and the cove once more.

Further yet, you join the principal road from Four Mile Bridge to Rhoscolyn village and the cove. The true Welsh name for Rhoscolyn is Llanwenfaen and the church is dedicated to St Gwenfaen, whose well we have already visited. There is a footpath from the church to Porth Saint, and another towards Borthwen

Holyhead Mountain: the main entrance to the ancient fort, breakwater in the distance

Holyhead Mountain from across Abraham's Bosom

Ruined boat-house at Penrhos
South Stack

which cuts several corners off the narrow, twisting lane.

RHOSCOLYN AND FOUR MILE BRIDGE

As there are no paths or rights of way directly between Four Mile Bridge and Rhoscolyn walkers are sometimes advised to take the road all the way. This is not a necessary evil! At GR 275773 a right of way on tracks crosses the road. If you go left (west) on this it takes you to Porth-y-garan, if you go right (east) you can get to Four Mile Bridge with no more road walking. This path will now be described fully, starting at Four Mile Bridge.

At the south-west end of Four Mile Bridge, by a house called Land's End, take a muddy path close to the water over boggy salt-marsh. This is signed 'Coastal path'. After about a quarter of a mile turn west, then south round a small inlet. (NOTE: *There is no coastal right of way south beyond here.*) Then go right over a stile (with notices: 'Dogs on Leads' and 'Beware of Adders') up between fences to a farm, Rhyd-y-bont (Ford Bridge). Go round to the back of the house on to the farm drive, past a large pond on your right. The farm drive swings sharply right by a dilapidated 'Nissen' type building, then bears a little left on to the road at GR 275773, as already mentioned.

Cross the road, over a stile, and straight up, right of a hedge, to a ladder stile in front of a holiday bungalow and continue to the road between Rhoscolyn village and Turnpike Farm. Cross this on to a farm-type drive, Bryn Ffysiwn. Soon after this pass Cerrig Moelion (Stony Hills) - appropriately named. When you reach a locked gate with a stile, marked 'Bryn Ffysiwn', with many prohibitions (private land), keep right of the mound on which the house stands and continue picturesquely to the junction with the coastal path at Porth-y-garan. (The 1:25,000 map shows the path crossing a series of small fields just here, but there seemed no sign of these on the ground.)

The South Coast

A glance at the map shows that Anglesey is divided by a series of parallel depressions, too shallow to be called valleys. Where not drained or flooded they are marshy. The main feature of the most northerly is Llyn Alaw, the largest lake in Anglesey, created in 1966 as a reservoir by flooding much of a huge marsh, Cors-y-bol. This gives rise to the Afon Alaw whose estuary is north of the Stanley Embankment. Part of the same system of marshes is Llyn Llywenan which is drained by the Afon Crigyll, whose waters reach the sea at Rhosneigr. Then comes the Cors (marsh) Bodwrog. Parallel to this and a little further south-east is the Afon Gwna which flows into Llyn Coron and emerges from it as Afon Ffraw, the eponymous river of Aberffraw. Even more significant is the huge strip, now largely drained, that runs from Malltraeth Sands to Red Wharf Bay, gathering *en route* the Afon Cefni, which flows through Llangefni from the Cefni Reservoir. This 'valley' at one time almost formed a strait, and the name 'Pentraeth' (Head of the Beach) shows how much nearer that village was to the waters of Red Wharf Bay.

Finally, we have the Afon (River) Menai, whose Welsh name shows that the Menai Strait can rightly be regarded as the largest and most southerly of this series of shallow valleys. It was indeed formed at the end of the last Ice Age by the flooding of the Cadnant Valley, thus cutting Ynys Môn off from the mainland and initiating its existence as an island.

The Menai Strait coast of Anglesey is full of features of major interest, but it nevertheless has less to offer the coastal walker than its three sister coasts. People wanting to walk around the whole island might do well to get this section out of the way first! Several parts of this coast are simply not worth recommending as Coastal Walks in their own right. However, the possibilities (and impossibilities) must be mentioned.

NEWBOROUGH TO THE MERMAID INN

There is no really satisfactory coastal walk between Newborough

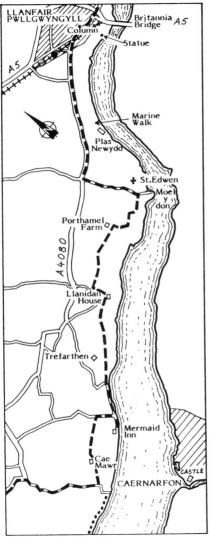

and the Mermaid. Some of the problems and difficulties to be described here may well change in time, but at present it is not fair actually to recommend any of the theoretically possible routes.

If you start at the sharp bend (with roundabout) (map p48) on the A4080 south of Newborough and walk a little way towards Bryn-siencyn there is a right of way down a narrow road on your right. (Factory Farming buildings on its left.) You can also drive down this cul-de-sac: very limited parking/turning space at the end. Beyond the drivable section there is a fence and wicket-gate through which a some-what overgrown path takes you to the Gate-houses Stepping Stones and Ford over the Afon Braint. When I encountered these recently more than half of them were missing or submerged and an attempt to cross the ford dryshod in wellingtons was unsuccessful. (At best some of the stones only 'surface' when the tide is very low.)

If in the future the stepping stones are restored the right of way beyond them goes left towards Dwyran: but when I looked at this there was a discouraging fence quite near the stepping stones. Some guidebooks suggest you go that way and then take the right of way through Cae'r-llechau. The path apparently goes through Cae'r-llechau's garden and parts of the route have been allowed to become so overgrown that a machete would be needed to get through!

An alternative, assuming you have got over the stepping stones or ford, would be to turn right along the left bank of the river. There is no right of way and it would be necessary to keep close to the river to avoid trespassing of land held by Rhuddgaer. However, once you reach the shore you are OK as long as you keep below the high-water mark (TIDE TABLES ESSENTIAL). In this way it is possible, though slow going, to get all the way to the Mermaid.

You will encounter another ford and at Menaifron you must go round or through a small private property with a bungalow, boathouse and disused harbour. Notice just before this the ruin of an old fisherman's cottage: one room only, but it did have a fireplace. The lady who now owns Menaifron says that when they were children they used to change in this when bathing. The next feature you pass is a Stud Farm and Riding Stables at Plas-y-borth. Less than a mile after this you reach the Mermaid, a welcome hostelry at the end of a cul-de-sac and with a magnificent view across the strait to Caernarfon Castle. When the tide is rising beware of being marooned on one of the many sandbanks.

If in the face of these dire warnings you are determined to walk to the Mermaid you must start on the main A4080 towards Dwyran. The road turns 90 degrees right at Ty Croes, by the church, and passes near the Bird World. At an acute bend left a minor road goes sharp right. Follow this. After a few hundred yards there is a 'No Through Road' on your right. Do not take this: it is where you would emerge if you did brave the Cae'r-llechau property. Nor is the right of way on your left a few yards further on ('Lodge' on OS map) any use to you. Keep on the road. Just past Tyn-y-goedan (GR 458645) your map tells you there is a right of way on the left which crosses fields diagonally to Cae-mawr (Big Field). At the time of writing there is no trace of this on the ground, but if by the time you are using this book it is signed as a footpath, use it. Otherwise continue on the road past Talgwynedd to a sharp right turn. Here you have a choice:

1) Continue on the road to its end. This is Plas-y-borth, the stud farm and riding centre already mentioned. Pass through this and turn left on the shore (if the tide is low enough) and proceed to the Mermaid.

2) Turn left up the farm drive to Cae-mawr. This is not a right of way, but I think you are unlikely to encounter trouble. Go straight past the farm (NOT sharp right, which is a right of way to the shore) and pick up the right of way that was not clear at Tyn-y-goedan. You will soon find good stiles and reassuring yellow waymarks. Pass on the left of Cerrig-y-barcud (Kite Stones) and reach the road where, perhaps to your surprise, there is a 'Coastal Footpath' signpost. (It is to be presumed that this section of path is one of the many that the local authority is gradually improving. Perhaps some parish councils have got on more quickly than others.) Walk down the road to the shore, and turn right if you want the amenities of the Mermaid.

The inn is on the site of a former ferry across the Strait. The site also has historical importance, as it may have been that of a famous battle in the year 1157.

In that year Henry II of England, concerned at the fact that the border of Gwynedd, under the powerful Owain Gwynedd, was too near the strategically important city of Chester for comfort, mounted a major military campaign against Gwynedd. The king's army advanced from Chester along the North Wales coast while a fleet sailed north from Pembroke to make a rendezvous with the king. On the way this fleet, for whatever reason, but anyway unwisely, carried out a raid on Anglesey and fought the Battle of Tâl Moelfre in which the English were heavily defeated by the men of Ynys Môn. Scholars are divided as to the actual site of this battle, usually assuming that it was the modern Moelfre on the east coast. But two poets who celebrated the victory, Gwalchmai and Hywel ab Owain Gwynedd, both refer to the Menai Strait, the former even describing with poetic hyperbole a 'great tide of blood' flowing into the Menai Strait. It is also significant that the Mermaid is situated at Tal-y-Foel (Foel being Moel by initial mutation), which could thus be identical with Tâl Moelfre. The

Welsh were less successful in fighting Henry II's army, though they nearly had a success near Hawarden, and Owain Gwynedd had to give up territory between the Clwyd and the Dee.

MERMAID INN TO MOEL-Y-DON

This rewarding walk, in some ways the best on the Menai Coast, can be started at the Mermaid where there is a car park, apparently public, just outside the private precincts. But remember that apart from the deservedly popular inn, there are two family attractions in this area - the Foel Farm and the Anglesey Sea Zoo (Sw Môr Môn). The latter certainly earns its place in the Top Ten attractions of North Wales and on holidays during the summer the traffic generated can be horrendous.

Walk along the coast road, but instead of turning sharp left towards Dwyran, continue by the shore on a minor road as far as Barras. Go in front of a house on to the foreshore and you will find a stile with a 'Coastal Footpath' sign. Following the path, and admiring Plas Trefarthen, a fine house, on your left, cross four fields. This brings you to a wall beyond which is a small wood. There are two gates and a stile. Take the stile. (You will find a yellow waymark at least on the far side, where there is also a stump with waymarks.) The little wood is rough and pleasant. (Avoid the disused quarry to the right.) Pick your way through: there is a waymarked stump to guide you. At the far side of the wood there is another stone wall with a high stile, interesting in that it has a gate on top, possibly to make it more sheep-proof. The right of way runs diagonally across the next field to a rather elaborate stile by a gate. (A sewage works has been built at the bottom of the field and a sewer to it has been laid. The rough fence and stile near the sewer are probably temporary.)

You are now at Llanidan. Walk down the road past the entrance to the sewage works. The road swings round to the left. But before you follow it spare a moment to look at the church. It is closed for restoration, but you can peep through gates at the ruin, of which the most striking part is the west end.

The church's patron saint is St Nidan, who worshipped at this site in the early 7th century. The ruin, of course, has a much later date, the 14th century. Part of it was demolished in 1844. It is not easy in the last years of the millennium to imagine this quiet spot, 'far from the madding crowd', as the centre of life for the whole Brynsiencyn area. It was Henry Rowlands (1635-1723), a rector here, who in his book on the ancient monuments of Anglesey, Mona Antiqua Restaurata, *perpetrated the error of associating these with druidism. He also wrote about farming methods.*

Now follow the road round to the left and you will soon reach a hard-top lane on the right with a 'Coastal Footpath' signpost. You are less than half a mile from the shore and high enough above it to get good views, so that this really gives a 'coastal' feeling. Soon you reach Bryn Llwyd. Here a signposted path comes down from the A4080. Shortly after this the hard-top lane turns right to Meini-gwynion Isaf, but the right of way continues straight on (no sign).

If you do this walk in springtime you will find a beautiful floor of wild garlic - ancestor of our cultivated onion, leek, garlic and chive - and bluebells. Early botanists, seeking a Classical origin for everything, called it a hyacinth, but a hyacinth non-scriptus *because it was not mentioned in the writers of Greece and Rome. It is in fact a flower belonging to the western fringe of Europe. We should be proud of it as a native beauty and in Wales perhaps use one of its Welsh names,* Croeso-haf *(welcome summer) or* glas y llwyn *(blue of the grove).*

Soon our lane is joined by another signed footpath from the A4080, this time down a green lane. (In 1997 there were no further signs on this route.) Soon the path turns right. Straight on is an old metal gate: obviously not the way to go. Very quickly now you are in Porthamel Farm with its duck pond. The map shows the path going clockwise round this, but in fact continue with the pond on your left and then turn sharp right on a further lane. At the next junction keep left, then right by a house, and bear left at another until you emerge on the hard-top road from Plas Cefn Mawr to Moel-y-don. (If you reverse this walk, note that there is no footpath sign at present at the end of the lane, only a 'No Through Road' sign.)

Whatever your plans after this, it is worth your while to walk down to Moel-y-don. You can have your picnic here.

There is no ale-house or café, but even on a cool and windy day it is delightful to look across to Y Felinheli and to imagine the ferry-boat which for hundreds of years left and arrived at the jetty here, and in particular to remember the Anglesey quarrymen who were ferried across to catch a train to the Dinorwig slate quarries, and the loads of slate similarly brought down for worldwide export, which gave Y Felinheli its modern name of Port Dinorwig. It is also possible that it was at Moel-y-don that Paulinus Suetonius landed his invading army in AD 60. Peter Sawley in his monumental volume Roman Britain *in* The Oxford History of England *does not commit himself to a landing-place, and perhaps it is my own innate Welsh romanticism that makes me prefer to visualise Tacitus' vivid account of the invasion as taking place on the dunes and mud-flats of Aber Menai.*

MOEL-Y-DON TO BEAUMARIS

Between Moel-y-don and Beaumaris there is no public coastal path, so this section of 'coast' can only be covered by road, some of it well inland. But there are major features of interest so, although this is not a guide to the tourist attractions of the island, these features must be pointed out and the route between them sketched.

From Moel-y-don go up the road to its crossing with the A4080. A narrow lane on the right a few hundred yards from Moel-y-don leads to the Church of St Edwen, picturesque in its setting of yew trees, although only comparatively modern: it was rebuilt in 1856.

At the crossroads turn right. After a good half mile you pass the entrance to Plas Newydd. If you are a member of the National Trust, entrance is free; if not there is an entrance fee for the gardens and house.

The house contains a celebrated mural, painted between 1936 and 1940 by Rex Whistler. Humphrey Repton's gardens of 1799 feature **The Marine Walk,** *discovered by one of the gardeners in the course of his work after its having been 'lost' for about a century. It was a favourite walk of one of the earlier Marquesses of Anglesey. It was reopened on 3 April 1997 to coincide with the National Trust's publication of the beautifully illustrated booklet* Rhyfeddodau Afon Menai: The Hidden World of the Menai Strait.

Go down in front of the house, walk as if to the Rhododendron Garden, then down to the shore. About half a mile has been cleared and made walkable so far, and Paul Carr-Griffiths, the Property Manager, tells me that the restoration will be further extended in due course. (He is especially enthusiastic about this discovery because there is so little access to the coast of the Menai Strait.) The Marine Walk provides one of the best viewpoints from which to admire The Britannia Bridge.

This bridge was in its day an engineering wonder, and those of us who are old enough can still recall it in its original, innovative form: two vast wrought-iron tubes which were self-supporting, without need for arches or suspension. It was designed by Robert Stephenson, son of George Stephenson of Rocket *fame, and William Fairburn. After 120 years of service from 1850 it was destroyed in 1970 by a disastrous fire in the highly combustible materials which lined the tubes, a fire caused accidentally by two boys who were looking for bats! In the reconstruction it was converted to a dual-purpose bridge for rail and road. To support the additional weight it is now furnished with arches and has lost the unique character of the original tubes. Perhaps it is symbolic of a cultural as well as technological change that when you drive a car over it today you are quite unaware of the older form of transport underneath the carriageway.*

Driving from the mainland over the Britannia Bridge you are struck by **The Anglesey Column**. This was erected in 1816-1817 to commemorate the 1st Marquess of Anglesey who was Wellington's second-in-command at the Battle of Waterloo.

Tradition has it that when a cannonball tore off his leg he merely said to Wellington, 'By God sir, I've lost my leg!' to which the Iron Duke simply replied 'By God, sir, so you have!' The Marquess's famous wooden leg, remarkable for being articulated, can be seen at Plas Newydd. He earned the nickname 'Old One Leg'. The column is 35m high and the view of Snowdonia from the top is ample reward for the effort of climbing its 115 steps. The rock on which the column stands tells us by its name, Craig-y-Ddinas, that it is the site of an ancient fort.

To reach the Column you will have had to pass the southern edge of Llanfairpwllgwyngyll or Llanfair PG as it is commonly called. (The lengthened name, Llanfairpwllgwyngyllgogery-chwyrndrobwllllantysiliogogogoch was a mere 19th century trick to achieve the longest placename in Britain for the benefit of tourists: the trick has certainly worked!)

The Church of St Mary from which the village takes its name (Llanfair means Church of St Mary) lies down near the shore, as does a statue of Nelson. (The village also has the honour of having seen the first meeting of the Women's Institute in Britain.) Continue on the A4080 to The Menai Suspension Bridge.

This bridge, only a mile by water from the Britannia Bridge, is the older of the two and, like the latter, is one of the world's engineering wonders, having been the first large iron suspension bridge in the world, designed by the great Thomas Telford in 1818 and opened in 1826. Despite strengthening and the replacement of the wrought-iron chains by steel, the bridge, unlike the Britannia, has retained its original character. In Welsh it is known as Pont Menai or Pont Borth. The latter name refers to the informal shortened form 'Borth' of the Welsh name for the town of Menai Bridge, which is Porthaethwy. Obviously the English name post-dates the building of the bridge. One of the major advantages to the islanders of the new bridge was that cattle going to mainland markets no longer had to swim the strait, with all the risks that involved.

The bridge, at that time the only one over the Strait, evidently made an impression on Lewis Carroll when he crossed it as a child. His White Knight in Through the Looking-Glass, *ever inventive,*

<blockquote>
had just
Completed my design
To keep the Menai bridge from rust
By boiling it in wine.
</blockquote>

(More practical than the Knight, the original engineers had treated the chains with oil.)

Do not miss going down under the bridge where there is a lane leading to a promenade dating from 1914-1916, when it was built by Belgian refugees, or go down through the woods, Coed Cyrnol. The situations are both dramatic and picturesque. Whichever way you go you will find the causeway leading to Ynys Tysilio or Church Island. This is a 'must' for all visitors to the area.

Although the present church of St Tysilio dates only from the 14th century, the saint himself, the son of one of the Princes of Powys, settled here in the 7th century and no doubt built himself a cell or church, probably of wood. Of course, he had no causeway to the mainland.

When the tide is running you will be impressed by the strength of the dangerous currents of the Swellies or Pwll Ceris in this narrow part of the straits. In 1953 HMS Conway *was wrecked here when under tow.*

Between Porthaethwy and Beaumaris there is no coastal path at all, but you can avoid the very busy A545 on a slightly more inland

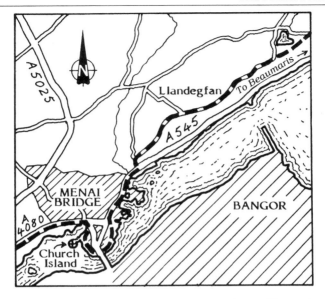

road which is also higher and gives some views. About three-quarters of a mile from the town centre, on the Beaumaris road, a modern bridge by-passes a sharp bend over the deep valley of the Afon Cadnant - the very river whose lower valley formed the Menai Strait. A few yards beyond this bridge, Pont Cadnant, go sharp left uphill and bear right with the road. You will pass the edge of a modern development, Llandegfan. (The old village is further inland.) After just under 2 miles there is a sharp bend left, and immediately after this a footpath on the right. It passes quite near the Llyn Pen-y-Parc reservoir and emerges on a road opposite a golf course. Go to the right on this road and you are soon in Beaumaris.

Beaumaris, as its very un-Welsh name implies, is not a native town but was founded by Edward I (1239-1307) after he had put down the Welsh revolt under Madog ap Llywelyn. In a decisive battle at Maes Moydog in Montgomery the Welsh were defeated.

On Anglesey two men, Goronwy and Trahaern, were responsible for hanging Sir Roger de Puleston, the sheriff of Anglesey, who is said to have

75

been unpopular and extortionate. One result was the burning of the town of Llanfaes and the forcible eviction of its inhabitants to Newborough. On 11 April 1295 Edward crossed from Bangor and made his headquarters at Llanfaes for three weeks, during which he gave orders for the town and castle of Beaumaris to be established.

Beaumaris Castle is a true 'picture book' castle to the eye. A visit to this is another 'must'. Its level site enabled it to be 'ideally' designed; it was close to the sea to which its moat was linked; and its design has a 'textbook symmetry' in terms of military architecture.

Its building (never actually completed) and its history, however, are anything but 'fairy tale'. Despite its design it was captured by Owain Glyndŵr in 1403 and held by the Welsh for two years. It was even involved during the English Civil War when General Thomas Mytton's Parliamentary forces captured it from Colonel Richard Bulkeley (Royalist) in 1646.

Beaumaris also has a Court House which until 1971 had the distinction of being the oldest building where Assize Courts were held. There is also a Victorian prison, complete with treadmill.

Until the building of the Menai Suspension Bridge the normal crossing to Anglesey, including that for travellers to Ireland, was to walk across Traeth Lafan at low tide and then take a ferry to Beaumaris. It was an uncomfortable and sometimes hazardous route.

BEAUMARIS TO PENMON

How satisfactory a coastal walk you can have between Beaumaris and Penmon depends entirely on the state of the tide. Using your tide tables try to arrange to do this walk at low tide, when it is well worth doing, with extensive views across Lavan Sands (Traeth Lafan), now a Nature Reserve, to the rolling skyline of the Carneddau on the mainland beyond.

From near the castle you can find a walk along the clifftops over the Mound. Then follow the road to the end of the pavement. If the tide permits turn right on to the foreshore.

The road that branches left here leads past some modern industrial and housing development to what is left of Llanfaes, the town depopulated by Edward I of England. There is a charming church, a few modernised

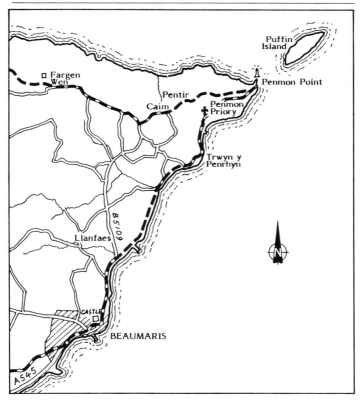

cottages and a yew-tree, the girth of whose trunk is so vast that it may well have witnessed the depopulation of the village in 1295.

If you have timed your walk correctly you can now keep on the foreshore all the way to Trwyn y Penrhyn (both elements in this name mean a headland!), roughly 2 miles: and it *is* 'roughly' in another sense, as you pick your way along the shore. There are 'escape' routes on to the road: one is at GR 618783, a right of way up a lane past Tre-Castell Farm; another is at GR 620791 at Cerrig (not named on OS map). A substantial flight of steps leads to a path that soon meets the road (limited parking). If the tide is too high all this must be done by road and therefore cannot be recommended as a coastal walk. From Trwyn y Penrhyn there is no choice but to use the road, but unless you have chosen a popular day you will find it quiet, and the view in front of you of the priory and its surroundings is peaceful and attractive.

PENMON

Although ill-served, thanks primarily to Penmon and Dinmor quarries, by actual coastal paths, and although it is most inconveniently cut off both on the 1:50,000 and 1:25,000 OS maps, the Penmon peninsula is one of the most interesting areas from a historical point of view in the whole of Anglesey.

As you approach along the coastal road from Beaumaris you will see first the Priory and Church and may well begin your explorations here; but for the moment let us proceed along the narrow road (toll for vehicles in the summer) to Trwyn Du (Black Headland), the most easterly point of Anglesey. Across a treacherous strip of water lies Puffin Island.

There are no puffins there now. Their extinction has been blamed on rats, but it seems equally probable that they were exterminated in the 19th century, when pickled puffin was regarded as a delicacy. The little island has been given many names: Ynys Lannog, for example, and Ynys Glannauc. Another name is Priestholm. This takes us back to the foundation of a religious settlement there in the 6th century by St Seiriol. Yet another name for Puffin Island is Ynys Seiriol.

Tradition has it that a certain Cynlas founded the religious house for his brother Seiriol. The remains of a rectangular enclosure, several monastic cells and a church survive. At the same time Seiriol had a cell on the mainland near the site of the later Priory, by a well of clear water, Ffynnon Seiriol (St Seiriol's Well). There is an 18th century brick shelter over the well.

St Seiriol, who was related to the royal family of Gwynedd, is one of the two patron saints of Anglesey. The other is St Cybi who is remembered in the Welsh name for Holyhead, Caergybi. An amusing, though doubtless apocryphal legend has it that these two contemporary saints used to meet at regular intervals at an agreed rendezvous. Seiriol had his back to the morning sun, and when returning in the afternoon had his back to the sun again, while Cybi faced the sun all day. Consequently Seiriol became

78

known as the White Saint, and Cybi as the Red. Seiriol was buried on Ynys Seiriol.

Despite the cars and the picnic-baskets, the former coastguard buildings, the modern coastguard station and the café, it is still possible to appreciate that Ynys Seiriol was once one of the holiest places in Anglesey. The strait between the headland and the island is guarded by a beacon on Perch Rock and a lighthouse on the mainland.

This has a bell whose mournful note sounds every 30 seconds, and it does not need much imagination to hear in this an echo of a medieval bell calling the monks to prayer. The lighthouse was built in 1837 and has a beam visible for over 13 miles. (There are also the ruins of a 19th century telegraph station on Puffin Island.)

The priory (Priordy Penmon), to which we must now return, dates from the 12th century. A former wooden church had been burnt down by invading Danes in AD 971.

The period during which the new, stone church was built was one of comparative peace and prosperity after Gruffydd ap Cynan had repulsed the Normans. Until about this time the Ynys Seiriol community had been in the form of a clas, *a monastic community of secular canons under an abbot. Then it became a regular house of Augustinians or Black Canons and was granted the church, which was probably extended at this time.*

A leaflet can be obtained giving details of the dates etc of the various features of the church. The 13th century chancel was rebuilt in 1855 and is used for normal services. Do not neglect to visit the refectory.

After about one thousand years of history the monastery, like most others, was dissolved in 1537 and was passed to the Bulkeley Estates. A.D. Carr in *Medieval Anglesey* remarks:

> On the evidence available it must be suspected that Penmon in the years before its dissolution was not a centre of spiritual endeavour. One has the impression that the prior and canons lived off their rents and enjoyed a moderately comfortable bachelor existence. (p.291)

Before leaving, look inside the elegantly dignified dovecote. It was probably built about 1600 for Sir Richard Bulkeley. It contains about a thousand pigeon holes. A stone pillar inside can be mounted by a primitive spiral step-way. From its top ladders could be extended to reach the pigeon holes.

In the 18th century the Bulkeleys created a Deer Park, part of whose wall we shall later follow. Meanwhile, within the bounds of the Deer Park, about 450yds west-north-west of the church (GR 625806) there is an ancient cross in a style partly Irish and partly Scandinavian. (It is marked on the 1:50,000 OS map but, oddly, not on the 1:25,000.)

It is thought to date from about the year AD 1000 and may have been a replacement for an earlier cross destroyed in one of the many Viking raids of the 10th century.

Traeth Abermenai (Newborough) with Snowdonia beyond
Beaumaris Castle

Penmon Priory and Columbarium
Penmon Point with lighthouse and Puffin Island

The East Coast

PENMON TO LLANDDONA BEACH

There is NO true Coastal Path between Trwyn Du (Penmon Point) and Llanddona Beach. (See map p77 for beginning of route)

From Trwyn Du take the path almost due west, pass a wall and reach a lane. If you turn right on this lane you get to Dinmor Park quarries. These, which were used during the construction of the A55 coastal expressway during the 1980s, are out of bounds even when not being worked. Trespassers find them extremely impressive. Non-trespassers should cross the lane. After another field a path to the left leads back to the toll road a few yards beyond the toll booth. Otherwise continue, bearing right a little and then left, outside the Deer Park, with its high wall on your left, until you reach Pentir.

Here there are two possibilities of a round walk:

1) a very sharp left brings you back to the priory;

2) less sharply left takes you through the Deer Park to Penmon village. If you turn left on the road you will soon reach stone steps in a high wall; from here a path follows a limestone ridge (good views) back to the priory.

If you are determined to visit every available bit of coast, turn right at Pentir. You will reach the coast but be unable to go on along it in either direction.

Straight ahead at Pentir is a narrow, twisty lane. This joins a slightly less narrow lane at a tiny hamlet called Caim. If you turn left on this road you will reach Penmon village and the paths already described. Just beyond the road-junction a track leads right to the coast: another cul-de-sac!

From this point it is probably best to endure road-walking for a time. Continue south-west to a T-junction at GR 616804, turn right and walk for about a mile. (To avoid this, Harry Ashcroft, *A Walker's Guide to the Anglesey Coastal Path*, suggests a rather complex route through lanes and fields.) At GR 602813 a right of way leads right to Fedw Fawr, a National Trust property where you are free to walk

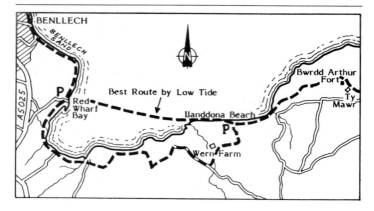

on the clifftops or go down steps to a pebbly beach. But this is yet another dead-end.

You must continue to GR 596813 where you will find on the right a conspicuous footpath sign by a gate and cattle grid. Take this until the farm track bends right, to Fargen Wen. Do not follow the track but go straight on until you find a ladder-stile at the junction of stone walls. Walking due west, then north-west, keep the wall on your left until you reach Ty-Mawr (Big House) where a ladder-stile is closely followed by two awkward stone stiles. You are now on a lane which provides vehicle access for Ty Mawr and also to a little church of Llanfihangel Din Sylwy that lies snugly under the eastern slopes of Bwrdd Arthur (Arthur's Table). Turn right on this lane and at the fork a few hundred yards further take the left, for Tan-dinas (Under the City), not the other, leading to Pen Maen (Head of the Stone).

Go straight through the farm, and shortly afterwards you are on open, rough country. Bwrdd Arthur, up on your left, is accessible from here. It is the site of Din Sylwy, the largest hillfort in Anglesey (in terms of area). It was probably first occupied about 300BC by Celts and was still in use at least until the Roman occupation. (Yet another public footpath comes down here from the road.)

A ladder-stile leads to a large field (keep the wall on your right) followed by yet another ladder-stile. Cross the corner of a field and over a stile - which actually has a small 'Coastal Footpath' sign on

82

it - into Bryn Offa (National Trust). Go down a path diagonally (easy this way, but not very obvious in reverse). It leads to a track and a stump whose waymarks will probably still be obliterated.

Keep on down to a house called Ty Llwyn. (A steep part of the track is concrete.) At Ty Llwyn there is a stump with several yellow arrows. If you keep left and pass between two houses, Pandy and Pentrellwyn, you come out on the road above Tywyn, go down the hill, past the church of St Dona (largely rebuilt in 1873), and turn right for the beach and coast road.

If you turn right at Ty Llwyn you come to a bungalow, Godreddi Mawr. Keep left over fields until at last, keeping outside a private garden, over a small stream, you will see the true 'Coastal Path' sign at the end of the beach. Notice the remains of an old fish weir, evidence of the former fishing industry.

LLANDDONA BEACH TO RED WHARF BAY

Llanddona Beach is not named on the OS maps. It takes its name from the village of Llanddona that lies above, about a mile inland. From the village, the beach (*traeth*) is well signposted, but if you are driving a car, be forewarned. There are three roads down to the beach, one from the direction of Bwrdd Arthur (gradient 25 per cent) and one from Llanddona, which forks before dropping down: the right-hand road has a gradient of 35 per cent(!) and the left-hand 25 per cent. This last leads most directly to the large car park, toilets and kiosk; for despite its relative inaccessibility Llanddona Beach is very popular.

Although Llanddona itself has little to attract a walker, it has a legend, or tradition, worth the telling, which may possibly have some basis in fact, connected with an actual shipwreck. The story is that a boat, wrecked in a storm in Red Wharf Bay, carried several red-haired, non-Welsh-speaking witches, who settled in Llanddona and were even given Welsh names. One was a dwarf with two thumbs on her left hand - a fact certain to arouse superstitious fears. Their smuggler husbands were also credited with unpleasant magical powers. To this day Llanddona people are sometimes nicknamed 'Llanddona witches' (gwrachod Llanddona).

Red Wharf Bay (in Welsh Traeth Coch - Red Beach), of which Llanddona Beach forms the eastern section, is the largest beach on

Anglesey. It must be treated with great respect, for although there is safe bathing at its edges, it is a labyrinth of tidal channels in which it is all too easy to be cut off on sandbanks.

(No one wants to suffer the fate of Charles Kinglsey's Mary who, when sent to call the cattle home across the sands of Dee, was caught by mist and tide, 'and never home came she'.) It is in fact perfectly possible at low tide to take a bee-line across the sands from Llanddona to the village of Red Wharf Bay (or even to the headland north of it), but it is about 3 miles of soft, sandy walking and involves some paddling. It should only be attempted by fit, fast walkers. You MUST consult the tide tables, and don't start later than 2 hours before the turn of the tide.

Alternatively you can walk *round* the bay. This is more like 5 miles. Some parts are extremely muddy and some are impossible at high tide. The following suggestions may help.

If you want to avoid the first muddy bit, walk up the Llanddona road from the car park to a track, with kissing-gate, on the right, at GR 568803. This takes you across fields and through some ancient woodlands to Wern y Wylan (hotel). Turn right on the road and walk to its end on the coast. You may prefer to take the muddy coast from here, or you may attempt to find your way along footpaths.

(Rights of way in wooded areas such as this of Mynydd Llwydiarth are very difficult to follow and are sometimes blocked. Forestry roads are almost equally unpredictable. If you encounter problems I suggest you return to the muddy shore!)

From the end of the Wern y Wylan road take a track inland to Côch y mieri and then, if possible, continue on the level past Ty-mawr. You are aiming for a bridge and telephone kiosk. (You may be told at Côch y mieri to go up through the woods. This is a nuisance, and you must find your way down again towards the bridge as best you can. It *is* possible.)

The Afon Nodwydd flows down from Pentraeth, whose name 'Head of the Beach' shows that at one time the sea must have come up the valley that far.

When George Borrow visited Pentraeth in 1854 on his way to visit the birthplace of the great Welsh poet, Goronwy Owen (1723-69), its full name was Pentraeth Goch. Meeting a poor old man by the stream in the village, Borrow asked him,

"To what place does this water run?"
"I know no Saxon," said he in trembling accents.
I repeated my question in Welsh.
"To the sea," he said, "which is not far off, indeed it is so
near that when there are high tides, the salt water comes up
to this bridge."

Wild Wales. Ch. XXXII

A few yards beyond the bridge a track leads to a right of way all the way up to Pentraeth. At high tide you may have to use this: it is a pleasant walk. At Pentraeth take the A5025 north until you reach a 'Red Wharf Bay' signpost and follow this road down to the village.

If the sea permits, however, follow the coast on tracks, until you reach the pretty and deservedly popular little village with its jetty, car park, hotels and refreshments.

RED WHARF BAY TO MOELFRE

Leave the actual village at the Ship Inn and walk due north along the beach. At low tide this presents no problems, but at high tide you must turn inland behind Castell Mawr and follow a track to the Caravan Park Clubhouse. Castell Mawr (Big Castle) is a most impressive natural fortress, surrounded by steep limestone cliffs, that was the site of a Celtic fort up to Roman times, though the ordnance map does not show it as such.

The headland, Trwyn Dwlban, which divides Red Wharf Bay from Benllech Sands, is occupied by a large caravan park whose privacy must be respected.

Although Benllech itself is a place to be avoided, its beach is magnificent, especially at low tide. You will probably find your route easier if you go up on to the Promenade towards the northern end of the beach. Go down from that northern end of the Promenade on the left of a stream that emerges from a tunnel under the road. Bear left on a roughly built rock and concrete path to the start of the cliff path, which runs between the cliffs and a sophisticated caravan site.

This is a fine path through stunted cliffside trees, where you usually see black-headed gulls, often black-backed gulls and, if you

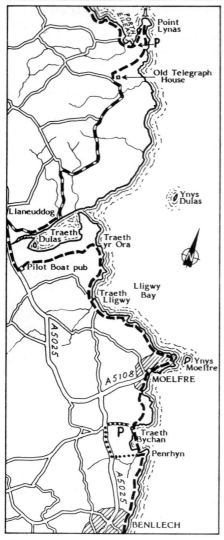

are very fortunate, a peregrine falcon. Unfortunately part of this section of the coastal path is vulnerable to dangerous erosion and twice in recent years has had to be closed until it could be re-routed a little further from the cliff-edge. The path drops a little by a camping field then climbs again to the vulnerable section until it reaches a bungalow, Nyth y'Wylan (Seagull's Nest), perched high above a very slightly indented cove, Borth Wen (White Port). Here a public footpath runs inland to the main road: useful if you are walking south on the cliff path and find that it has collapsed once more south of Nyth y'Wylan. Continue along the cliff path until it turns right and drops a little to a south-facing viewpoint (iron railing protection). Keep to the right of a ruined, perhaps military, building, and keep to the coast (dogs on leads) round

Penrhyn, the headland that forms the southern tip of Traeth Bychan (Small Beach). Pause to speculate on the origin of a vast pyramid of, apparently, quarried rocks. Does it represent an aborted jetty or fortification? You are now on the property of Penrhyn Caravan Park, most of which is out of bounds.

At the gated slipway used by the caravan park you have, tide permitting, a choice. If the tide is low you can walk all the way along the beach to the northern end; if the tide is rather higher you will be forced to undertake a rocky scramble; if it is too high even for this you must turn inland - *not* through the caravan site, but up a path and then a lane to the main road. Turn right on this until you reach the signpost to Traeth Bychan about 1km further on. Turn right down this to pick up the coastal path again.

Traeth Bychan is virtually monopolised by a yachting club, but there is a good car park if you want to start a walk from here, and seasonally a small shop.

Beyond Traeth Bychan the coastal path crosses several fields - often quite muddy - until it picks up a farm track at Nant Bychan (Small Stream) which takes you down to Moelfre Harbour (Porth Moelfre) by the Kinmell Arms. Parking here is very limited, but there is more in the town.

Walk round the harbour, then go right, keeping as close to the sea as possible. You soon pass behind the old lifeboat house and then the new lifeboat house. Just before you reach this, notice up on your left a modern glass-fronted building with a lifeboat inside! This is the Centre of Sea-life and History, set up by Anglesey Coastal Heritage. To visit this you need to go up to the road and to hope that you are there at the correct season, the right day and the right time of opening!

MOELFRE TO LLIGWY

Moelfre Lifeboat has a long and heroic history, recorded on the inner walls of the lifeboat house and celebrated in the new museum. Continue past the lifeboat house. Across the sound (Y Swnt) you cannot but notice Moelfre Island (Ynys Moelfre), always fully inhabited by seagulls and cormorants. Turning left you must walk almost on the edge of the beach past the end of a charming little row of bungalow-cottages, until you reach a kissing-gate where the footpath sign directs you up to the Coastguard Lookout, now, sadly, out of use; but to make the most of the coast keep to the right and walk round the headland, which on the map is oddly called Eglwys Siglen, The Church in the Bog, though no vestige is to be seen of either bog or church. The coastal view from here stretches from Point Lynas to the Great Orme.

Just beyond the Coastguard Lookout footpath signs painted on rocks show an alternative way into the town. The Coast Path continues, however, past kissing-gates and stiles, to the edge of a caravan park magnificently placed on the slopes and escarpment above Porth Halaeth, into which you now drop. The path here has been immensely improved in recent years by volunteer labour.

You will by now have spotted a simple stone memorial (surrounded, quite unnecessarily, by an iron railing) standing on a craggy outcrop above the far side of this little stony beach. It is reached over a stile. Erected in 1935 it commemorates the most celebrated of the many wrecks that have occurred on this dangerous coast, that of the *Royal Charter*.

The Royal Charter *belongs to a special time in the history of shipbuilding, a time when iron was replacing wood and steam replacing sail. It was a type of ship that might well have never been developed but for the Australian Gold Rush which began in 1851 and which led to a demand for fast passenger ships capable of circumnavigating the globe without the benefit of the Suez and Panama canals. Described in its advertisements as a "Magnificent Steam Clipper", she was a three-masted, full-rigged ship of 2719 tons, with an auxiliary steam-engine of 200hp which was only to be used when wind-power failed, especially in the Doldrums. Its hull was of iron and its design based on that of the wooden-hulled sailing clippers, long and narrow, like a canoe or a Viking longship. Within, it was, at least for the First Class passengers, a floating hotel with many luxuries and a menu worthy of any onshore establishment.*

At the time when she made her last and fatal voyage the Royal Charter *had already become famous: she had reached Melbourne in just under 60 days, at a time when the normal passage was over 90. On this trip home she was carrying gold to the value of £322,440 (a vast amount in those days) as well as the personal fortunes, also in gold, of many of her 390 passengers. (There was also a crew of 112).*

Having left Melbourne on 26 August 1859 she arrived at Queenstown, Ireland after a non-stop voyage on 24 October, and it was almost certain that she would again reach Liverpool in under 60 days. As she passed Holyhead Island between 4 and 5pm the next day there was a strong south-east wind blowing. No one in 1859 could have foreseen what was coming, namely the worst storm of the century, in which 133 ships were sunk, 90 badly damaged and about 800 lives lost, over half of them in this very ship. At about 10pm the wind unpredictably (in those days) changed to east-north-east at Force 10, quickly rising to an incredible Force 12, thus driving the ship directly towards the north-east coast of Anglesey. At 3.30am, in total darkness, the ship struck. She split in two, leaving most of the passengers stranded on one section. No women and children survived. Eighteen male passengers appear to have survived, and of 11 riggers taken on board near Bardsey Island, 5 survived. Of the crew of over 100, only 18 survived - none of them officers.

There is no doubt that before the site could be satisfactorily sealed off, a good deal of gold had, illegally of course, found its way into the pockets of Moelfre villagers. Nor did the search for gold end then. Groups of salvors, sometimes in fierce rivalry, have continued up to the present day, especially after the wreck of the 650-ton Hindlea, *on 27 October 1959, one hundred years and a day later, had again drawn attention to the wrecked 'treasure ship'.*

Leaving the site of the wreck, follow the path above cliffs which, though not high, are impressive as natural fortifications. Fishermen frequent the rock pavements below, and fulmars nest in the ledges where the coast bends sharply into Porth Forllwyd, a private cove belonging to the Moryn Estate, which you pass along a field path.

You are now looking at Traeth Lligwy, one of the most extensive beaches on the island. If the tide is low enough you will see below you a curved line of boulders which, though almost 'natural', gives the impression of being an unfinished breakwater. The feature is marked *Gored* on the map, apparently the mutated form of *Cored*, meaning a weir or dam, so is presumably man-made.

Lligwy Beach is privately owned above mean high-water mark, so there are restrictions on dogs above that mark, and the car parks at each end of the beach are liable to have a charge. There is also a shop, open seasonally, and public toilets which are open sometimes.

About half a mile inland from Lligwy Beach are three of the most interesting archaeological remains on the island, spanning between them some 4000 years of history: Lligwy Burial Chamber, which dates from Neolithic times, perhaps 4000 BC, with its huge capstone; Din Lligwy, a village that was probably walled in the 4th century after the Roman withdrawal and whose square-built houses, among the more usual round ones, suggest Roman influence; and Hen Capel Lligwy (Lligwy Old Chapel), parts of which go back to the 12th century. This extraordinary group of remains is well worth visiting if your time permits.

Lligwy Beach can be approached from Llanallgo crossroads on the road which passes these ancient monuments, or by road from Bryn Refail; or by footpath down Nant y Perfedd. The latter two both lead to the car park at GR 493872.

LLIGWY TO DULAS

After crossing the sands you begin the next lap from the car park. The path leads past some picnic tables and continues, up and down, near the cliff edge. You will pass a tower-like brick structure, probably of military origin, and come out on a small headland, Trwyn Porth-y-Môr. At low tide you can walk as far as this on the sands and get up with a bit of a scramble.

At Porth-y-Môr (Sea Port) itself the path goes down on to the beach. A footpath (stile) comes down here from the minor road to Brynrefail. Soon the coastal path goes up again, keeping outside the fenced field. At a further stile you are on an open field. This is part of a private (club) campsite based on Penrhyn. Signs request you to keep near the edge and not to trespass further inland. Bearing left you find yourself looking down on Traeth yr Ora, a most attractive beach, but often empty of visitors because of its inaccessibility.

At the end of the field there is a private path on the left, and a stile on the right. Beyond the stile, steps lead down to the beach. If you keep up above the beach you find a seat and a sign directing you inland up a track. This is the most direct way to continue the coastal walk, virtually blocked as it is by the Dulas Estuary. The track goes round the Penrhyn Campsite and joins the cul-de-sac road from Brynrefail. When this turns sharp left by a house, follow the signed

Stranded boat at Dulas Estuary

footpath round the house. This continues across the fields, well signed on posts, until it reaches the Pilot Boat Inn on the main road.

You will see on your left a monument on a small eminence. There is a path to this from the main (A5025) road (memorial stone and kissing-gate). This monument, a Celtic cross, commemorates the four Morris Brothers, Lewis (1701-65), Richard (1703-79), William (1705-63) and John (1706-40).

All were men of high culture, true representatives of the Age of Enlightenment. Lewis was a cartographer, historian and linguist. Himself a writer of prose and poetry, he also encouraged the work of a younger poet, Geronwy Owen (1723-69), "Geronwy Ddu o Fôn" (Black Geronwy of Anglesey), still remembered for his little Welsh quatrain in praise of his native island. Richard, a collector of folk-songs, was important in his influence on Welsh culture, particularly on the Welsh living in London, among whom he founded The Honourable Society of Cymmrodorion (fellows, consociates). William was a botanist and literary enthusiast, as was John, who was killed fighting in Spain.

If you do not go inland by the seat you can continue (no sign) along an isthmus between Traeth yr Ora and Traeth Dulas. Where this widens in a promontory (cultivated field, keep to the edge) you can either go on and find a place to scramble down on to the salt-marsh or go left down a rough and muddy path (and this *does* have a footpath sign) also on to the foreshore. A lot depends here on the state of the tide.

At high tide the estuary forms a picturesque lake, with the decaying remains of long-abandoned hulks; at low tide there are extensive sands cut through by the course of the Afon Gôch. When the tide is running there is a quite spectacular tidal race in the narrow entrance to the estuary. And always this area is a haunt of birds.

You can follow the southern shore of the estuary (sometimes boggily) to where the rough road past Glan-Traeth (Shore of the Beach) comes down from Brynrefail. This runs straight into the water.

Looking across the estuary you can see that this is exactly opposite a road which comes down past the church (spire) and similarly runs straight into the water. Clearly this was once a ford, but definitely not to be attempted in a vehicle today. At very low tide I have seen a man cross it on foot, but I greatly doubt whether he did it dryshod!

Throughout this walk you will no doubt have been intrigued by Ynys Dulas (Dulas Island) with its strange tower. This was built by the lady of the manor in the 19th century both as a seamark and as a place of refuge for sailors. Emergency supplies were stored in it.

DULAS TO POINT LYNAS

From the Pilot Boat Inn there is, at least at present, no satisfactory footpath with a continuous right of way to the other side of the estuary. It is best to walk to Llaneuddog and take the lane on the right (east). This goes down by Gwaith Bries and a small lake (parking here). Now you can walk, boggily in places, along the shore past Coch-willan-bach to the end of the road that comes down from the church. (There is no parking and virtually no turning for cars here.)

At exceptionally high tides it may be necessary to walk on the A5025 beyond Llaneuddog and take the next road on the right - near '54' on the map. At the sign 'Private' ahead turn sharp left, then right at a T-junction. This brings you to the top of the road past the church. Fork right to visit the shore or left to continue towards Point Lynas.

There is NO coastal footpath most of the way between the Dulas

Estuary and Point Lynas, and walkers must use the road - fortunately a fairly quiet one but not to be recommended as a 'coastal walk'.

For scramblers - and I emphasise *scramblers* - it is possible to get along below high-water mark, and therefore legally and without trespassing.

This expedition has been vividly described by Roger Redfern in The Guardian (A Country Diary, 14.9.1996. *He is full of praise for this 'unmatched' and 'delectable' corner of Anglesey, but he firmly mentions 'scrambling' and 'one or two airy traverses round rock spires and hanging buttresses' as well as the danger of being cut off by the tide.*

Walkers must follow the road up by the spired church to the first road junction. Turn right, pass Plasuchaf (Upper Hall) and continue with the Llysdulas (Dulas Hall) Estate on your right; then follow the road round to the left. Ignore all paths or tracks to the right even if marked as rights of way on the map. At GR 481918 a path signposted 'Coastal Path' does in fact lead down to the coast, but there is no coastal path either way when you get there.

Go on to GR 479921. Here you will find a footpath sign at a lane on the right with the notice 'Old Telegraph House'. Go down here past some buildings. Pick up a track on the right and then follow a footpath down through fields to the coast and past Porth y Corwgl (Coracle Cove), round a headland with an offshore rock, Ynys Drai, then west across the peninsula to the road just outside the gates of Point Lynas lighthouse.

FURTHER READING

The Anglesey Guide. Môn Mam Cymru.
(The official guide to Anglesey. Beautifully produced. Fully illustrated. A mine of information.)

Snowdonia, Anglesey & the Lleyn Peninsula Walks. Pathfinder Guide (OS). Compiled by Brian Conduit.
(Contains 2 walks on Anglesey: Newborough & Moelfre)

Short Walks to Explore Anglesey. Kendell & Bradnam.
(19 walks)

A Walker's Guide to the Anglesey Coastal Path. Harry Ashcroft.
(Brief & clear guide to walking anti-clockwise round the island. Loose-leaf binding so that sections can be detached.)

Walking Anglesey's Coastline. John L. Merrill.
(Brief & clear guide to walking clockwise round the island.)

Anglesey. Guide to Walks. E. Rowlands.
(Contains many walks, coastal and inland. Very detailed.)

RSPB Guide to Bird Watching on Anglesey & Lleyn.
(The best sites and which birds you see.)

A Birdwatcher's Guide to Anglesey. R.E. Hutson
(Similar material. Only Anglesey.)

Wild Wales. George Borrow.
(19th century tour on foot. Includes a visit to Anglesey.)

Medieval Anglesey. A.D. Carr. Anglesey Antiquarian Society.
(Scholarly. Specialised.)

Anglesey. The Island's Story. Michael Senior. Gwasg Carreg Gwalch.
(A clear history in 64pp. Well illustrated.)

The Golden Wreck. The tragedy of the Royal Charter. Alexander McKee. Hodder & Stoughton.
(Comprehensive. Compelling. Well illustrated.)

The Hidden World of the Menai Strait. National Trust.
(A beautifully produced little book.)

Two Bridges over Menai. Robin Richards.
(The construction and story of Telford's bridge and the Britannia Bridge.)